English for Life

Pre-intermediate

Student's Book

Tom Hutchinson

Contents

BAT9150, 3WKS L28. 24. ENG

1a `1.1` **Read and listen. Where are Michael and Zofia from?**

Michael Hi. My name's Michael.

Zofia Pleased to meet you, Michael. I'm Zofia.

Michael Sorry. What's your name again?

Zofia It's Zofia – Z-O-F-I-A.

Michael Oh, OK. Nice to meet you, Zofia.

Zofia Where are you from, Michael?

Michael I'm from Canada. And you?

Zofia I'm from Poland.

Michael Oh, really? Whereabouts?

Zofia Krakow. Do you know it?

Michael Yes, I do. I was there last year with my wife.

b **Work with a partner. Practise the conversation.**

Language note *Whereabouts?*	
A Where are you from?	**A** Where is she from?
B I'm from Italy.	**B** She's from New York.
A Whereabouts?	**A** Whereabouts?
B (I'm from) Rome.	**B** (She's from) Brooklyn.
Whereabouts? means 'Where exactly?'.	

2 `1.2` **Listen. Michael introduces a woman to Zofia. Choose the correct answers.**

1 She's
   a his boss.
   b his wife.
   c his girlfriend.

2 Her name is
   a Mia.
   b Soshi.
   c Olivia.

3 She's
   a Polish.
   b Canadian.
   c Chinese.

3 Your life **Greet some people in your class. Use the conversation in exercise 1.**

4a Write the countries.

Country	Nationality
Poland	Polish
Canada	Canadian
_____	Chinese
_____	Brazilian
_____	Irish
_____	Greek
_____	Russian
_____	American
_____	French
_____	Egyptian
_____	Japanese
_____	Spanish

b `1.3` **Listen, check, and repeat.**

5 `1.4` **Drill. Listen. Say the nationalities.**

1 Hello. I'm Felipe. I'm from Brazil.
   His name's Felipe. He's Brazilian.

1 Felipe   2 Effie   3 Akira

4 Kate   5 Ahmed   6 Olga

6 Your life **Work in a group of three. Introduce each other. Follow the pattern.**

A Hi, Niran. This is my friend, Judit.

B Pleased to meet you. Sorry. What's your name again?

C It's Judit. Nice to meet you, too.

A Niran's from Thailand.

C Oh, really?

B What about you, Judit? Where are you from?

C I'm from Hungary.

B Oh, that's interesting.

✓ Now I can ... *introduce people and name some nationalities.*

1a Complete the questions. Choose the correct words.

Who are you?

Name _____ **Answer**

1 Where *am/is/are* you from?
2 What *'m/'s/'re* your last name?
3 *Am/Are/Is* you married?
4 When *have/is/are* your birthday?
5 Where *are/was/were* you born?
6 *Have/Has/Do* you got any brothers and sisters?
7 *Has/Have/Do* you got a car?
8 *Are/Do/Does* you live near here?
9 What *are/do/does* you do?
10 What *do/are/have* you do in your free time?

b `2.1` **Listen and check.**

2 Read the examples. Study the rules on page 103.

Question forms: *be, have got, do*
Are you from France?
Where **are you** from?
Have you got any children?
How many children **have you got**?
Do you live in Paris?
Where **do you** live?

3 `2.2` **Drill. Listen. Say the question.**

1 You're a student.
   Are you a student?
2 You've got two children.
   Have you got two children?

4 Ask a partner the questions in exercise 1. Write down his/her answers.

A *Where are you from?*
B *I'm from …*

5a Change the questions to *he/she*. Write them down.

1 Where are you from?
   → *Where is he/she from?*

b Work with a new partner. Ask and answer about your first partners.

6 Writing Write a paragraph about yourself. Change the words in bold.

My name's **Maria** and I'm from **Italy**. I'm **married** and my last name is **Valerio**. I was born in **Naples** and my birthday is on **14 August**. I've got **two brothers and one sister**. I live **outside Naples** now **with my husband and two children**. I'm **a secretary** and I **work in an office**. At weekends, I **go cycling with my family**.

Pronunciation
The phonemic alphabet

1 `2.3` **We use a phonemic alphabet to show pronunciation (see page 124).**

	/sʌn/	/sʌn/
different letter, same sound:	sun	son
	/kʌm/	/həʊm/
same letter, different sound:	come	home

2a Choose the correct word to match the phonemic transcription.

1 /lʊk/	like	look
2 /nəʊ/	know	now
3 /wiːk/	week	work
4 /mæn/	man	men
5 /jɔː/	you	your
6 /eɪt/	eat	eight

b `2.4` **Listen, check, and repeat.**

 Now I can …
ask about and give personal information.

1 `3.1` **Listen. Meryem is registering at a language school. Choose the correct answers.**

1 She's *Turkish / Egyptian*.
2 She's a *doctor / chemist*.
3 She's *single / married*.
4 She *has / hasn't* got children.
5 Her address is in *Brighton / London*.
6 She gives a *mobile / daytime* phone number.

2a Use your answers to exercise 1. Complete those parts of the form.

Global Language School

Personal details

Title:	*Ms*	Gender:	Female ✓ Male
First name(s):			
Surname:		Date of birth:	
Nationality:			
Occupation:			
Marital status:	Single Married Separated Divorced Widowed	No. of dependants:	

Contact details

Address

House number:		Street:	
Town/City:		Postcode:	

Telephone/email

Tel. no: (daytime)		(evening)	
Mobile:		Email:	

b Listen again. Complete the rest of the form.

3 Match the 'official' terms with the questions.

1 Surname *f*
2 Age ___
3 Nationality ___
4 Date of birth ___
5 Marital status ___
6 No. of dependants ___
7 Address ___
8 Occupation ___

a How old are you?
b Where do you live?
c When were you born?
d What do you do?
e Are you married?
f What's your last name?
g Have you got any children?
h Where are you from?

> **Language note**
> **Giving your date of birth**
>
> 16 March 1985
> **We write:** 16.03.85
> **We say:** sixteen (oh) three eighty-five
> OR
> the sixteenth of the third eighty-five

4 Speaking Use the form in exercise 2 and the questions in exercise 3. Interview your partner.

> **English in the world**
> Saying email addresses
>
> **1 Say the email addresses below.**
> meryem.yilmaz@abc.com
>
> *meryem dot yilmaz at a b c dot com*
>
> a_person@anywhere.co.uk
>
> *a underscore person at anywhere dot co dot u k*
>
> z-antonio@abbi.pt
>
> *z hyphen antonio at abbi dot p t*
>
> **2 How do you say email addresses in your language?**

> Now I can ... *give information about myself and complete a form.*

1 `4.1` **Read and listen.**

My name's Lucy Patterson and I'm British. I work for an advertising agency. I'm a personal assistant. This is my boyfriend. His name's Jordan Morris and he's Australian. He's a computer engineer, but he really wants to be an actor.

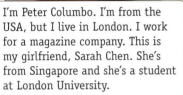

I'm Peter Columbo. I'm from the USA, but I live in London. I work for a magazine company. This is my girlfriend, Sarah Chen. She's from Singapore and she's a student at London University.

My name's Cindy Gaskell and that's my husband, Ryan. I'm from Britain, but Ryan is from Ireland. This is our Internet café. We've got two children. Melanie is 21 and Russell is 24.

2 **Read the texts. Copy and complete the table.**

	Name	Nationality	Job
1	Lucy Patterson	British	personal assistant
2			

3 **Complete the sentences with the correct names.**

1 _____ is Ryan and Cindy's son.
2 _____ is Jordan's girlfriend.
3 _____ is Ryan's wife.
4 _____ is Sarah's boyfriend.
5 _____ is Russell's sister.
6 _____ are Melanie's parents.

4 `4.2` **Read and listen to the story. Answer the questions.**

1 Why is Peter busy?
2 Where is Sarah?
3 Who is at university in Manchester?
4 Where is Russell at the moment?

Cindy Morning, Peter. How are you?
Peter Fine, thanks, Cindy. And you?
Cindy Yes, OK. Are you busy?
Peter Yes, I am. We're moving to our new offices this week.
Cindy How's Sarah? Is she away at the moment?
Peter Yes, she's in Manchester.
Cindy Really? Our daughter, Melanie, is at university there.
Peter How's your son these days?
Cindy Russell? I don't know. He's travelling round the world. He was in Mexico last month.

Arrival of flight VK964 from Mexico City.

Oh, it's good to be home!

5 **Complete the expressions.**

Everyday expressions Asking about people

How _____ you?
Are _____ busy?
How_____ Sarah?
Is she _____ at the moment?

6 **Work in a group. Practise the story in exercise 4.**

 Now I can ... *ask how people are and what they're doing.*

5 VOCABULARY
Jobs

1 5.1 **Listen and repeat.**

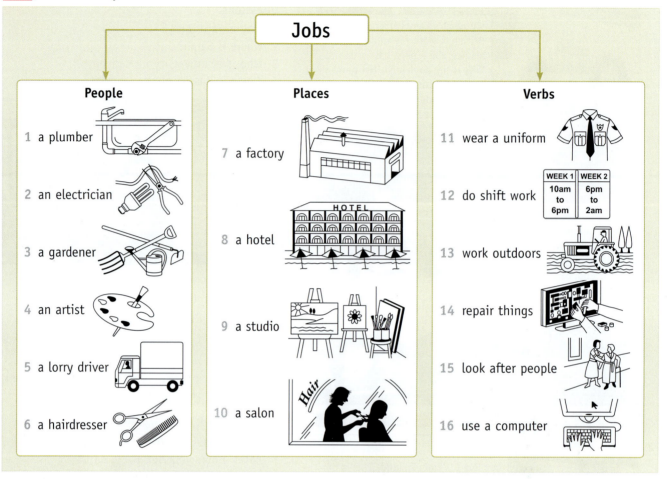

Jobs

People

1 a plumber
2 an electrician
3 a gardener
4 an artist
5 a lorry driver
6 a hairdresser

Places

7 a factory
8 a hotel
9 a studio
10 a salon

Verbs

11 wear a uniform
12 do shift work
13 work outdoors
14 repair things
15 look after people
16 use a computer

2 Add two people, places, and verbs to the diagram.

Language note Word building 1		
I drive a lorry.	→	I'm **a lorry driver**.
I clean windows.	→	I'm **a window cleaner**.

3 Give two examples of people who do the things in the VERBS section of the diagram.

wear a uniform: *police officers, flight attendants*

4 Write three sentences about each person below.

– *He/She's a …*
– *He/She works (in a) …*
– *He/She does/uses, etc. …*

5 Work with a partner.
A Think of a job.
B Ask questions.
A Answer: *Yes, I do.* OR *No, I don't.*
B Try to guess the job.

A *Do you wear a uniform?*
B *No, I don't.*
A *Do you work in a … ?*
B *Yes, I do.*
A *Are you a … ?*

6 **Writing** Write eight sentences about your job/studies and your friends/family.

1 *I'm an electrician. I work in a hospital. I repair …*
2 *My sister is an artist. She works in a studio in the city. She draws …*

| ✓ | Now I can …
name and describe different jobs. |
| --- | --- |

6 GRAMMAR
Present simple

1 **6.1** **Read and listen. Who is Russell talking about?**

Russell	Hi, Dad. Can I ... Mmm, she's nice. **Does she come** here every day?
Ryan	Lucy? **Yes, she does. She** usually **comes** in when she finishes work.
Russell	**Does she work** near here?
Ryan	**No, she doesn't**, but **she lives** near here – in Brent Street.
Russell	Oh, right. **What does she do**?
Ryan	**She works** for an advertising company. **Do you like** her?
Russell	**Yes, I do. I think** she's gorgeous.
Ryan	Well, **she doesn't need** a boyfriend, I'm afraid. She's already got one. It's Jordan.
Russell	Oh!

2 **Read the examples. Study the rules on page 103.**

Present simple	
We use the present simple for:	
permanent states She **lives** near here.	
regular activities She **comes** here every day.	
I **live** in Brent Street. I **don't work** near here.	She **lives** in Brent Street. She **doesn't work** near here.
Do you **come** here every day? Yes, I **do**. No, I **don't**.	**Does** she **come** here every day? Yes, she **does**. No, she **doesn't**.
Where **do** you **work**?	Where **does** she **work**?

3 **Describe Jordan's life.**

1 He lives in Park Road.

1 I live in Park Road.
2 I work for a computer company.
3 I repair computers.
4 I drive a van.
5 I start work at nine o'clock.
6 I finish work at 5.30.
7 I often go to The Coffee Shop.
8 I meet my friends there.

4 **6.2** **Drill. Listen. Say the negative.**

1 I live near the station.
   I don't live near the station.
2 He finishes work at six.
   He doesn't finish work at six.

5 **Ellen is talking about her life. Complete the text with the verbs in brackets.**

I ¹ *work* (work) in an old people's home and I normally ²_____ (work) at night. My husband, Dave, ³_____ (work) in an office. He ⁴_____ (not work) at night. I ⁵_____ (finish) work at 7 a.m. and I ⁶_____ (get) home at 7.15. I ⁷_____ (not take) the children to school. Dave ⁸_____ (take) them and I ⁹_____ (go) to bed. Dave ¹⁰_____ (finish) work at 5.30. We ¹¹_____ (have) a meal together. At 10.30, I ¹²_____ (drive) to work. Dave normally ¹³_____ (watch) TV for an hour and then he ¹⁴_____ (go) to bed.

6a **Speaking** **Make questions for Ellen. Use the cues.**

1 Where / you / work?
2 you / work / at night?
3 What / your husband / do?
4 he / work / at night, too?
5 What time / you / finish work?
6 What / you / do / during the day?
7 What time / Dave / finish work?
8 What / you / do / in the evening?

b **Work with a partner. Ask the questions and give Ellen's answers.**

7 **Your life** **Write a paragraph about your daily life. Use some of the verbs below.**

work   get up   have   leave   drive
start   finish   go   watch

Now I can ...
talk and ask about people's working lives.

1 **7.1** **Read and listen to the text. What does Arne do? Does he like his job?**

My job

Arne Henriksen lives in a village near Stavanger in Norway. He's an electrical engineer and he works on an oil rig in the North Sea.

Arne lives on the rig for two weeks and then he has two weeks off. For the first week, he's on the day shift from 7 a.m. to 7 p.m. In the second week, he changes to the night shift.

When he isn't on duty, he always sleeps a lot. He usually goes to the gym, too, and he sometimes plays table tennis. There's a cinema on the rig, so Arne normally watches five or six films a week.

About 480 people work on the rig. It's like a small village with all sorts of workers – cleaners, engineers, plumbers, electricians, chefs, secretaries, computer engineers, nurses, painters, and so on.

After two weeks, Arne leaves the rig and goes home. 'We have a small farm, so there are always things to do,' he says. He doesn't usually work all the time when he's at home. He likes fishing, and in the winter he often goes skiing.

Arne likes his job. The money is very good and he enjoys the time at home, but there are problems. 'The weather's often bad in the North Sea, so the rig moves a lot,' he says. 'I rarely get seasick, but it isn't very nice when I do. The biggest problem is the shift work. When I change from the day shift to the night shift, I can never sleep. I watch a lot of films then!' ●

2 **Are the statements true (T) or false (F)?**

1 He lives in Norway.
2 He goes home every day.
3 He always works on the day shift.
4 A shift is twelve hours.
5 Over four hundred people work on the rig.
6 They're all engineers.
7 Arne works in a shop when he's at home.
8 He doesn't often get seasick in bad weather.

3 **Find these things in the text.**

– three things he does when he isn't on duty
– three other jobs that people do on the rig
– two things he does when he's at home
– two things that he likes about the job
– two problems with the job

Language note	Adverbs of frequency

0% ◄---► 100%
never   rarely   sometimes   often   usually / normally   always

He **sometimes plays** table tennis.
There **are always** things to do.
He **doesn't usually work** all the time.

4 **Make sentences with the adverbs of frequency about:**

1 Arne's life
2 your own life

5a **Speaking** **Write six questions to ask Arne.**

Where do you work?
Do you do shift work?

b **Work with a partner. Interview Arne.**

> ## English in the world
> ### 24/7
> ....
> Normal working hours in Britain are 9 a.m. to 5 p.m. However, a lot of people work outside these times because their workplaces are open 24/7 – twenty-four hours a day, seven days a week. For example:
> 1 hospitals, power stations, the police
> 2 bars and clubs
> 3 a lot of big supermarkets.
>
> **Compare this with your country.**

✓	Now I can ...
	ask about and describe someone's job.

1 Say these dates.

1 the first of May OR *May the first*

1 1 May
2 16 November
3 12 April
4 22 October
5 30 March
6 4 July
7 3 January
8 10 December
9 31 February

2a `8.1` **Listen and complete the dialogue. Use *in*, *on*, *at*.**

Receptionist Hello, Abbey Dental Practice.

Caller Hello. I've got an appointment ¹___ 1 June, but I'm afraid I can't make that now.

Receptionist I see. What time is your appointment?

Caller It's ²___ 12.45.

Receptionist Ah, yes. Mrs Henderson?

Caller Yes, that's right.

Receptionist Would you like to make a new appointment?

Caller Yes, please.

Receptionist Can you come ³___ 16 June ⁴___ the morning?

Caller What day is that?

Receptionist It's a Tuesday.

Caller Yes, that's fine. What time?

Receptionist Well, can you come ⁵___ half past ten or ⁶___ quarter past eleven?

Caller Oh, er, quarter past eleven, please.

Receptionist Fine. So your new appointment is ⁷___ 11.15 ⁸___ Tuesday 16 June.

Caller Thank you very much. Goodbye.

Receptionist Goodbye.

b Listen again and check.

c Work with a partner. Read the conversation.

3a Study the rules.

Prepositions of time: *in*, *on*, *at*		
in	1969	January
	the morning	winter
on	6 August	Sunday
	Friday afternoon	
at	six o'clock	3.15
	the weekend	night

b `8.2` **Drill. Listen. Say the sentence.**

1 When's your interview? (Friday)
It's on Friday.

4 Complete the expressions.

Everyday expressions
Making appointments

What time ____ your appointment?
I'm afraid I ____ make that now.
Would you like to ____ an appointment?
Can you ____ on 16 June?
What day ____ that?

5a `8.3` **Listen. Complete the table.**

		1	2
Old appointment	Date		
	Time		
New appointment	Date		
	Time		

b Work with a partner. Use the table above. Make the conversations.

Pronunciation
Word stress 1

1 `8.4` **Listen. Underline the syllable with the stress.**

Monday
July
afternoon
November
birthday
electrician
appointment

evening
Wednesday
April
receptionist
engineer
eleven
interview

2 Listen again and repeat.

✓	Now I can ... *make appointments.*

1a Write the verbs in the correct spaces below.

> have   do   get   make   go

1 _____ → shopping
2 _____ → out
3 _____ → to bed

4 _____ → a shower
5 _____ → breakfast
6 _____ → a rest

7 _____ → up
8 _____ → dressed
9 _____ → home

10 _____ → a cup of coffee
11 _____ → the bed
12 _____ → an appointment

13 _____ → my homework
14 _____ → the ironing
15 _____ → the housework

b 9.1 Listen, check, and repeat.

2 9.2 Drill. Listen. Say the sentence with the correct verb.

1 a shower
   I have a shower.
2 the housework
   I do the housework.

3 Make three expressions with each verb.

watch: *watch a football match, watch a DVD, ...*
listen to:
read:
play:

4a Use suitable verbs. Complete what Arun says about his day.

I ¹_get_ up at 7.30 and I ²_____ a shower. Then I ³_____ dressed and I ⁴_____ the bed. I ⁵_____ breakfast and I ⁶_____ the radio. Then I ⁷_____ to work. I ⁸_____ lunch at one o'clock. After work, I sometimes ⁹_____ shopping or I ¹⁰_____ tennis with some friends. When I ¹¹_____ home, I ¹²_____ dinner. I sometimes ¹³_____ some housework in the evening. I ¹⁴_____ the news on TV and then I ¹⁵_____ to bed. I ¹⁶_____ a book for a quarter of an hour before I ¹⁷_____ to sleep.

b 9.3 Listen and check.

5a Speaking Write six questions for your partner. Use the expressions from exercises 1–3.

Do you ... ?
When do you ... ?
Where do you ... ?

b Work with a partner. Ask and answer. Find two things that are the same.

6a Your life Choose two things that you:
– do every day
– never do
– normally do at the weekend
– like doing
– don't like doing.

b Write a sentence about each thing.

Pronunciation
Stress in expressions

1 **9.4 In expressions, we don't normally put the stress on the verb. Read and listen.**

• • ●
go to bed   • • ●
             have a shower

2 **9.5 Listen and repeat.**
get ready   have breakfast   go to work
make an appointment   read a book
play the piano   do the ironing

 Now I can ... *talk about everyday activities using collocations.*

1 `10.1` **Read and listen.**

Monday **wasn't** a good day for Lucy. Everything **went** wrong. She **was** in a hurry because she **got up** late. She **didn't have** breakfast. She just made a cup of coffee, but it was very hot and she **dropped** it.

She picked up her bag and her keys. Just then the post **arrived**. She put her keys on the table in the hall and **opened** the letters. There **were** two bills and a letter from the bank. She **left** the house, closed the door and **hurried** to her car. She stopped and looked in her bag. Her keys **weren't** there. And they weren't in her pocket. Then she remembered. They were on the table in the hall. And it wasn't just her car keys. Her house keys were there, too. It wasn't a good start to the week.

2a Read the examples. Study the rules on page 104.

Past simple: *to be*	
She **was** in a hurry.	Monday **wasn't** a good day.
There **were** two bills.	Her keys **weren't** there.

b Underline **more examples of the past simple of *to be* in the text.**

3 **Choose the correct form of the verb.**

1 Lucy's neighbours had a key, but they *wasn't/weren't* in, because they *was/were* on holiday.
2 The weather *wasn't/weren't* very good. It *was/were* cloudy and it *wasn't/weren't* very warm.
3 She walked to the bus stop, but there *was/were* a long queue and the first two buses *was/were* full.
4 Lucy *was/were* late, so her boss *wasn't/weren't* very happy.
5 In the afternoon Lucy *was/were* tired. She had three meetings. They *was/were* very long and boring.

4a Read the examples. Study the rules on page 105.

Past simple	
We use the past simple for completed events in the past.	
1 regular verbs	
open	I **opened** the letters.
2 irregular verbs (see page 123)	
get up	You **got up** late.
3 negative statements	
I had breakfast.	I **didn't have** breakfast.
NOT I didn't had breakfast	

b Underline **more examples of past simple verbs in the text in exercise 1.**

5 **Correct the sentences about Lucy's day.**

1 She didn't get up on time. She got up late.

1 She got up on time.
2 She had breakfast.
3 She drank a cup of coffee.
4 She picked up her laptop.
5 She put her keys down because the phone rang.
6 She got five bills in the post.
7 She left her keys in the kitchen.

6 `10.2` **Drill. Listen. Give the negative.**

1 I got up late.
I didn't get up late.

7a Put the verbs in the past simple.

1 I _was_ late for work. (be)
2 I _____ the bus. (take)
3 I _____ my keys. (lose)
4 I _____ ill. (be)
5 I _____ to the cinema. (go)
6 I _____ a DVD. (watch)
7 I _____ a pizza. (eat)
8 I _____ a bill. (get)

b Your life **Did these things happen to you yesterday? Tell a partner.**

I was late for work. OR *I wasn't late for work.*

✓	Now I can ... *talk about events in the past.*

1 Look at the pictures of Vijay and Seema. What is happening in each picture?

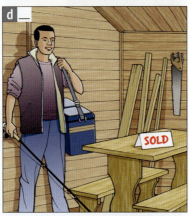

2 11.1 **Listen. Number the pictures in the correct order.**

3 Listen again. Answer the questions.

1 Why weren't Vijay and Seema happy?
2 Why did they have an argument?
3 Why did Vijay stop to talk to the man?
4 Why wasn't the man at work that day?
5 Where do Vijay and Seema live now?
6 What does Seema do?
7 What does Vijay do?
8 Why isn't he working today?

4 How did the conversation change Vijay and Seema's life? Complete the table.

Their life before	Their life now
They lived in a big house.	They live in a small village.
	He doesn't earn much money.
	He sees his family a lot.
	He works at home.
	He doesn't travel much.
	They're happy now.

> **Language note** *because* and *so*
>
> He was often away, **because** he travelled a lot. (reason)
>
> He travelled a lot, **so** he was often away. (result)

5 Writing Complete the summary of Vijay and Seema's story.

At first, life was good for Vijay and Seema. Vijay had a good job. He earned ¹_____, so ²_____. However, they weren't happy, because ³_____. When they were on holiday, Vijay phoned ⁴_____, so ⁵_____. Vijay went for a walk on the beach and he met a man. The man made ⁶_____ and he was very happy. Vijay and Seema decided to change their life, so ⁷_____.

Now Seema ⁸_____. Vijay ⁹_____, but he isn't working today, because ¹⁰_____.

> ## English in the world
> ### Moving house
>
> Most people in Britain own their house or flat. They usually take out a **mortgage** to pay for it. When they move house, they sell their house and buy another one.
>
> People normally buy and sell houses through an **estate agent**. A **solicitor** deals with the contracts and other legal matters.

> ✓ **Now I can ...**
> *understand and re-tell a story.*

1 Look back at Episode 1 on page 4.

   1 Where was Sarah last week?

   2 Who came home?

2 `12.1` Read and listen to the story. Does Russell help his parents in the café?

3 Are the statements true (T) or false (F)? Correct the false statements.

   1 Ryan is happy.

   2 Ryan and Cindy made a lot of money last month.

   3 The weather wasn't very good last month.

   4 The factory closed down a year ago.

   5 The workers don't go to the café any more.

   6 Russell arrived yesterday.

   7 He came home because he didn't have any money.

   8 Cindy's happy because Russell is at home.

   9 Russell always gets up at nine o'clock.

  10 Russell eats a lot.

4a Complete the expressions.

> **Everyday expressions**
> **Responding to information**
>
> Oh, I s_____.
> That's t_____.
> Yes, I h_____ about that.
> Oh, r_____.
> Yes, I see what you m_____.

b Practise the expressions together. Use the correct statements from exercise 3.

   A *Ryan isn't happy.*

   B *Yes, that's true.*

5 Language check. <u>Underline</u> examples of the past simple in the story.

6 Work in a group. Practise the story.

Sarah	Hello, Ryan. You don't look very happy.
Ryan	No. Well, we didn't make much money in the café last month – again.
Sarah	Oh, I see.
Ryan	We didn't get many customers, because the weather was bad. And the factory on the corner closed recently, so the workers don't come now.
Sarah	That's true.
Ryan	And last Thursday our son Russell arrived home.
Sarah	Yes, I heard about that.
Ryan	He was in Mexico, but he didn't have any money, so he came back.
Sarah	Oh, right.
Ryan	Cindy's happy. Russell can't do anything wrong in her eyes.
Sarah	But can't he help in the café? You could save some money.
Ryan	Russell? He doesn't get up till midday. And he eats like a horse!

No, you don't save money when Russell's here. You lose it.

Yes, I see what you mean.

Russell	Morning, Dad. Oh, hello.
Ryan	Russell, this is Sarah.
Sarah	Hi. Nice to meet you!
Ryan	And, it's the afternoon, actually.
Russell	Oh, OK. Can I have this coffee? And those cakes and sandwiches look good.

Now I can ...
respond to what people say.

1 13.1 **Listen and repeat.**

1 be born

2 grow up

3 move (house)

4 take an exam

5 graduate

6 get a job

7 lose a job

8 meet your future husband/wife

9 go out with someone

10 fall in love

11 get married

12 have children

13 get divorced

14 retire

15 die

2a Put the expressions in the table below.

general events	be born, …
education	take an exam, …
relationships	meet your future husband/wife, …
work	get a job, …

b Which verbs in the expressions have a regular past form?

3 13.2 **Drill. Listen. Say what happened last year.**

1 I / retire
  I retired last year.

> **Language note Years**
>
> **We say:**
> 1969 nineteen sixty-nine   2012 twenty twelve
> 2003 two thousand and three   1905 nineteen 'oh' five

4 13.3 **Listen. Bernard is talking about his life. Complete the sentences.**

1 His parents _____ in Chile.
2 Bernard _____ in Liverpool.
3 He _____ in London.
4 He _____ university in Birmingham.
5 He _____ his wife in Sydney.
6 He and his family _____ to South Africa.

5 Listen again. What does Bernard say about these numbers and dates?

1940s	1951	5
16	1969	1972
1980	35	2001

6a Your life **Write six sentences about your life story.**

b Tell a partner.

> **English in the world**
> **Going to university**
>
> University courses in Britain and the USA usually last three or four years. Students don't always go to their local university. They can choose any university in the country, so a lot of students go to a different city.
>
> First-year students normally live at the university in a hall of residence. In their second and third year, they often share a house or flat with other students.
>
> **Compare this with your country.**

✓ **Now I can …**
talk about a life story.

1 `14.1` **Read and listen.**

Bob How **did you meet** your husband, Sue?

Sue Well, it started in Rome.

Bob **Were you** on holiday?

Sue Yes, **I was**. Anyway, I saw this guy.

Bob **Was he** on holiday, too?

Sue No, **he wasn't**. He was a tour guide there.

Bob Oh, I see. So **did you go** on a date?

Sue No, **we didn't**. We didn't speak much, but two years later I saw him again – at our local supermarket.

Bob Really! What **did you do**?

Sue I said, '**Were you** a tour guide in Rome?' and he said, 'No.' It wasn't the same guy!

Bob Oops! **Did you tell** him about the tour guide?

Sue Yes, **I did**, and we laughed about it. Anyway, now we're married with three children.

2 **Read the examples. Study the rules on page 105.**

Past simple: questions and short answers	
1 The verb *to be*	
Were you on holiday?	Yes, we **were**. No, we **weren't**.
Was he a tour guide?	Yes, he **was**. No, he **wasn't**.
How long **were** you there?	
2 Regular and irregular verbs	
Did you **enjoy** your holiday?	Yes, I **did**. No, I **didn't**.
NOT ~~Did you enjoyed your holiday?~~	
What **did** he **say**?	

3 `14.2` **Drill. Listen. Ask the questions.**

1 We met in Paris.
Did you meet in Paris, too?

2 We were on holiday.
Were you on holiday, too?

4a **Complete the questions and short answers. Use the words in brackets.**

A [1](you / away) *Were you away* last week?

B [2](Yes) *Yes, I was*. I was in Moscow.

A Oh? [3](you / there) on business?

B [4](No). I was at my brother's wedding.

A Really? [5](he / marry) a girl from Russia?

B [6](Yes). Her name's Hanja.

A [7](they / meet) in Moscow?

B [8](Yes).

A [9](your brother / on holiday) there?

B [10](No). He was a student at Moscow University.

A [11](Hanja / a student) there, too?

B [12](Yes).

A [13](Why / he / go) to Moscow University?

B He studied Russian there.

A [14](you / visit) other places in Russia?

B [15](No), but I saw a lot of Moscow.

A [16](you / have) a good time?

B [17](Yes). I really enjoyed it.

b **Work with a partner. Practise the conversation.**

5a **Complete the questions. Use the verbs in brackets.**

1 Where ___*were you*___ born? (be)

2 _____ there ? (grow up)

3 _____ house when you were a child? (move)

4 Where _____ to school? (go)

5 _____ a good student? (be)

6 What subjects _____? (like)

7 How old _____ when you left school? (be)

8 _____ to university? (go)

b `Your life` **Use the questions in exercise 5a. Ask and answer with a partner. Try to find some more information.**

1 *Where were you born?*
Were your parents born there, too?
How long did you live there?

Now I can ...
ask questions about events in the past.

1 15.1 **Listen. Do you know these kinds of music?**

1 classical music   4 country music
2 jazz   5 soul
3 blues   6 gospel

2 15.2 **Read and listen to the text.**

The Father of Soul Music

Ray Charles Robinson was born in 1930 in Georgia, USA, but he grew up in Florida. He lived with his mother, Aretha, and his younger brother. They were very poor. When Ray was five years old, his brother died and then two years later Ray went blind. Aretha Robinson sent her son to St Augustine's, a school for blind children. He studied classical music there.

When Ray was fourteen, his mother died and he left school. For two years he played the piano with some local bands to earn the money for a bus ticket to Seattle. There he played in clubs and bars. He didn't earn a lot of money, but he loved music.

'Music,' he said, 'was like food or water for me.'

At first he sang songs by other famous singers, but he soon created a new kind of music. He used blues, jazz, country, and gospel music and he created 'soul music'. He changed his name to Ray Charles, and by 1955 the poor black boy from Florida was rich and famous.

He gave a lot of his money to schools for blind black children. His life also had a dark side. He took heroin for many years. He was married and divorced twice and had twelve children.

In 1988, a film director, Taylor Hackford, started planning a film about the singer's life. He called it *Ray*. The film's star, Jamie Foxx, won the Oscar for Best Actor in 2005. Sadly Ray Charles wasn't there. He died in June 2004 at the age of 73.

3 **Match the names with the descriptions.**

1 Jamie Foxx ___
2 Taylor Hackford ___
3 Ray Charles ___
4 Aretha Robinson ___

a directed the film *Ray*.
b was 'the father of soul music'.
c was the star of the film *Ray*.
d was Ray's mother.

4 **Read the text again. Put these events in the correct order.**

___ He went to St Augustine's School.
___ Jamie Foxx won an Oscar for Best Actor.
___ He moved to Seattle.
_1_ His brother died.
___ Taylor Hackford started a film about Ray.
___ He went blind.
___ He became rich and famous.
___ Ray Charles died.
___ His mother died.

5 **Answer the questions.**

1 Where was Ray Charles born?
2 Where did he grow up?
3 What did he study?
4 How did he travel to Seattle?
5 How did he save money for the ticket?
6 What did he say about music?
7 How did he create 'soul music'?
8 Who did he give money to?
9 How many children did he have?
10 How many times was he married?

> **Language note** **Infinitive of purpose**
>
> He played the piano **to earn** money for a bus ticket.
> He went to St Augustine's **to study** music.

6 **Speaking** **Work with a partner. Interview Taylor Hackford about Ray Charles' life. Use the questions in exercise 5.**

7 Your life **Think about your favourite singers and/or bands. What do you know about them? Tell a partner.**

> ✓ **Now I can ...**
> *talk about a famous person's life story.*

1a `16.1` **Read and listen. Match the conversations with the correct endings.**

1

I took my driving test yesterday.

How did it go?

a I passed.

Well done! I knew you could do it.

b I failed.

Never mind. Better luck next time.

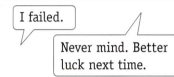

2

I had an interview for a job last week.

How was it?

a It was OK, but I didn't get it.

Oh, dear. Never mind.

b Great. I got it!

That's fantastic news!

3

I played in a tennis competition yesterday.

How did you get on?

a I won.

Congratulations! Well done!

b I lost.

Oh, dear. That's a pity.

b Work with a partner. Practise the conversations.

2 Complete the expressions.

Everyday expressions News

Asking about news
How did it _____?
How did you _____ on?
How _____ it?

Responding to good news
Well done!
I _____ you could do it.
That's _____ news!
Congratulations!

Responding to bad news
Never mind.
Better _____ next time.
Oh, dear.
That's _____ pity.

3 Make new conversations for these situations.
1 You had an audition last week.
2 You played in a sports match yesterday.
3 You took an English exam two weeks ago.

4a Read the email.

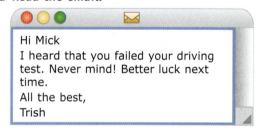

Hi Mick
I heard that you failed your driving test. Never mind! Better luck next time.
All the best,
Trish

b Write an email to 'Sam'. He passed his test.

5 Writing Look at situations 2 and 3 in exercise 1. Write emails to the people.

Pronunciation
Intonation

`16.2` **Listen and repeat.**
1 Well done! (good news)
2 Never mind (bad news)
3 Congratulations!
4 That's fantastic news!
5 Better luck next time.
6 I knew you could do it.
7 Oh, dear. That's a pity.

Now I can ...
ask about and respond to news.

1 17.1 **Read and listen.**

A Hello. Can I help you?

B Yes. How much is a ticket to London, please?

A **Single** or **return**?

B Return, please.

A OK. Well, **the fare** in **standard class** is £24 and the **first-class** fare is £46.

B And how much is **a seat reservation**?

A Seat reservations are free.

B And what time is the first train this afternoon, please?

A There's a train at 12.32, but that's **a local train** so it stops at every station.

B What time does it **get to** London?

A It arrives at 2.20.

B Is there a fast train?

A Yes. There's **an express** at 1.15 and that arrives in London at two o'clock.

B Oh, I think that's better.

A But the express isn't **direct**. You **change** at Oxford.

B Oh, OK. What platform does that train leave from?

A It **departs from** platform 3.

B Thank you very much.

2a **Match the meanings with the words in bold in exercise 1.**

1	a slow train *a local train*	7	the price of the ticket
2	a fast train	8	a seat that is booked
3	leaves from	9	non-stop
4	arrive in	10	take two trains
5	a one-way ticket	11	a cheap ticket
6	a two-way ticket	12	an expensive ticket

b **Practise the conversation with a partner.**

3a 17.2 **Listen. Are the statements true (T) or false (F)?**

1 The passenger wants to travel to Manchester.
2 She wants a standard class ticket.
3 She's travelling today.
4 She buys a return ticket.
5 She doesn't ask for a seat reservation.
6 The fare is £52.
7 The next train is direct.
8 There's an express at 11.30.
9 It arrives at 12 o'clock.
10 It leaves from platform 4.

b **Listen again and check.**

4a **Writing** **Use the information in exercise 1. Complete the email.**

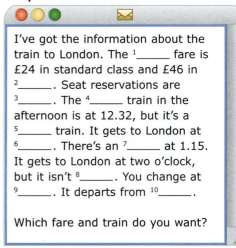

I've got the information about the train to London. The [1]_____ fare is £24 in standard class and £46 in [2]_____. Seat reservations are [3]_____. The [4]_____ train in the afternoon is at 12.32, but it's a [5]_____ train. It gets to London at [6]_____. There's an [7]_____ at 1.15. It gets to London at two o'clock, but it isn't [8]_____. You change at [9]_____. It departs from [10]_____.

Which fare and train do you want?

b **Write an email with the information in exercise 3.**

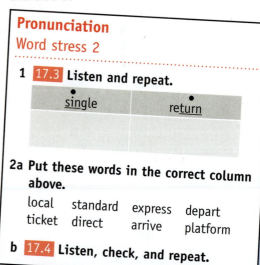

Pronunciation
Word stress 2

1 17.3 **Listen and repeat.**

•	•
single	return

2a **Put these words in the correct column above.**

local	standard	express	depart
ticket	direct	arrive	platform

b 17.4 **Listen, check, and repeat.**

✓ Now I can ...
talk about train journeys.

1 18.1 **Read and listen.**

Sarah is going to the university. She normally cycles, but she isn't cycling today because it's raining. At the moment, she's walking to the bus stop. Jordan is putting things in his van.

Sarah Hi, Jordan.

Jordan Oh, hi Sarah. **Are** you **going** to the university?

Sarah Yes, I am. I**'m not taking** my bike today, because I don't want to get wet.

Jordan Good idea.

Sarah What **are** you **doing**?

Jordan I**'m delivering** some computers. Nowhere near the university, I'm afraid, so I can't give you a lift.

Sarah Oh, that's OK. Bye.

Jordan Yes, see you. Don't get wet!

Oh! Jordan!

2 **Read the examples. Study the rules on page 106.**

Present continuous	
I**'m going** to work. He**'s taking** the bus. We**'re getting** in the car.	I**'m not walking**. She **isn't cycling**. They **aren't stopping**.
Are you **going** to the university?	Yes, I **am**. No, I**'m not**.
What **are** you **doing**? Where **is** she **going**?	

3a 18.2 **Listen. Write two sentences. Use the cues.**

1 She isn't cycling. She's walking.

1 she / cycle / walk
2 he / do a crossword / read a book
3 they / swim / jog
4 snow / rain
5 they / play golf / sunbathe
6 she / go to sleep / wake up

b **Ask and answer about the sentences above.**

A *Is she cycling?*   **B** *No, she isn't.*

4 **Read the examples. Study the rules on page 106.**

Present continuous and present simple
We use the present continuous for what is happening now. She **isn't cycling** today because it**'s raining**.
We use the present simple for regular activities. She usually **cycles** to the university.

5 **Put the verbs in brackets into the correct form.**

1 I usually *walk* (walk) to work, but I *'m not walking* (not walk) today. I _____ (take) the bus, because my bag's heavy.
2 We _____ (travel) to work by train every day. At the moment we _____ (stand) on the platform. We _____ (wait) for the 7.45 train, but it's late.
3 I usually _____ (go) to work at eight o'clock, but I _____ (leave) home early today, because they _____ (repair) the road at the moment.
4 Sandra usually _____ (get) to work at nine o'clock, but it's 9.15 now and she _____ (not sit) at her desk. She _____ (look for) somewhere to park.

6 Your life **Use the time expressions. Write six sentences about your life.**

I always have a shower in the morning.
I'm not having a shower at the moment.

always	every day	usually
at the moment	today	now

✓ **Now I can ...**
compare regular and current activities.

1 19.1 **Listen to three taxi conversations. Where is each passenger from?**

Euston Station, please.

2 Listen again. Complete the table.

Conversation	Destination	Fare
1	*Euston Station*	
2		
3		

3 Listen again. Which passenger is it? Write 1, 2, or 3.

_____ is travelling on business.
_____ gives the driver a tip.
_____ wants a receipt.
_____ likes the city.
_____ is on holiday.
_____ gets out of the taxi early.

Language note *want, like, need*

We don't normally use the present continuous with *want*, *like*, **and** *need*.

What number do you want?	NOT ~~What number are you wanting?~~
Do you like it there?	NOT ~~Are you liking it there?~~
You **need** International Departures.	NOT ~~You're needing International Departures.~~

4 Tick ✓ the things the taxi driver talks about. What does he say about them?
– the traffic
– sport
– his girlfriend
– the airport
– his family
– his job
– the weather

5 Speaking Make conversations in a taxi. Follow the pattern.
A Taxi! **Baker Street**, please.
B OK.

Talk to the passenger. Choose one of the topics in exercise 4.

B Here we are, **Baker Street**. What **number** do you want?
A **Number 29**, please.
B OK. Here we are – **number 29**.
A Thank you.
B That's **£8.50**, please.
A Could I have a receipt, please?
B Certainly. Here you are.
A Thank you very much. Goodbye.
B Bye.

English in the world
Transport signs

What are these signs in your language?

1 Roadworks

2 Crossroads

3 Dead end

4 Steep hill 10%

5 No entry

6 Sharp bend

✓ **Now I can ...** *listen for specific information in an informal conversation.*

1 **Look back at Episode 2. What does Ryan think about Russell?**

2 **20.1 Read and listen to the story. Who is the woman with the camera?**

3 **Answer the questions.**
1 What are Ryan and Russell doing?
2 Is it Ryan's idea?
3 What is Russell looking at?
4 Is The Coffee Shop open?
5 What is the woman doing?
6 Why does the woman ask about the area?
7 Where are Russell and the woman going?
8 Why is Cindy annoyed?

4a **Complete the expressions.**

> **Everyday expressions**
> **Offering and asking for help**
>
> Would you like _____ hand (with ...)?
> No, _____'s OK, thanks.
> Can you _____ me a hand with (...) ?
> Sure.
> I can ... if you _____.
> That's _____ kind. Thank you.

b **Work with a partner. Make conversations with the cues below. Start like this:**

Would you like ... ?
OR
Can you give ... ?
– the shopping
– these drinks
– the housework
– these bags
– the dinner

5 **Language check. <u>Underline</u> examples of the present continuous in the story.**

6 **Work in a group. Practise the story.**

1 *Sunday morning...*

Jordan Hi, Ryan. What are you doing?
Ryan We're putting tables and chairs outside the café. It's Cindy's idea.
Jordan Would you like a hand?
Ryan No, it's OK, thanks. Russell's helping me.
Jordan Oh, OK. See you, then.
Ryan Yes, bye, Jordan. Come on, Russell. What are you looking at?
Russell I'm looking at that woman over there with the camera.
Ryan She's probably a tourist. Anyway, can you give me a hand with this table?
Russell Sure ... Oh, just a minute. She's crossing the road. Mmm. She's very nice.

2

Woman Excuse me. Is The Coffee Shop open?
Ryan Yes, it is, but we aren't serving drinks outside at the moment.
Russell You're taking a lot of photographs. Are you a tourist?
Woman No, I'm not. I want to open a shop and I'm looking for a good area. What's this one like?
Russell Well, I'm not doing anything at the moment. I can show you around if you like.
Woman That's very kind. Thank you. I'm Anna, by the way.

3 Come on, Ryan! Why aren't you moving those tables? Hurry up!

Now I can ...
offer and ask for help.

1 **21.1** **Listen and repeat.**

1 along the street

2 round the park

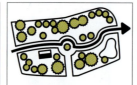

3 through the park

4 over the bridge

5 under the bridge

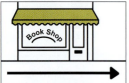

6 past the shop

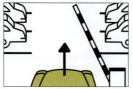

7 into the car park

8 out of the car park

9 up the hill

10 down the hill

11 at the end of the road

12 in the middle of the square

13 on the corner of the street

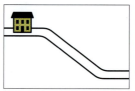

14 at the top of the hill

15 at the bottom of the hill

2 **21.2** **Drill. Listen. Give the opposite.**

1 Go over the bridge.
No, go under the bridge.

2 Turn left.
No, turn right.

3 **21.3** **Listen. Which building is Magda's office? A, B, C, or D?**

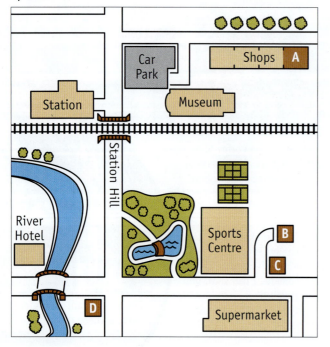

4 **Speaking** **Ask for directions from the station to these places. Use the map in exercise 3.**

– the park
– the sports centre
– the River Hotel
– the museum

A *Excuse me. How do I get to the park, please?*
B *You turn right here, then you go under the bridge. After that, you … .*

5 **Your life** **Describe your route to work or school.**

I come out of my flat and I turn right. I go down the stairs. At the bottom of the stairs, I turn left …

Pronunciation
of short form

1 **21.4** **Listen. In expressions, we normally reduce *of* to a schwa /ə/ sound.**

/əv/
It's in the middle of the town.

/əv/
It's at the top of the hill.

2 **21.5** **Listen and repeat. Copy the stress.**

1 It's at the end of the road.
2 It's on the corner of the street.
3 It's at the bottom of the hill.
4 It's in the middle of the square.

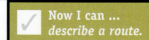

Now I can …
describe a route.

1a 22.1 **Read and listen.**

Martin	When I **was going** to the cash machine, I saw a man and a woman.
Policeman	**Were they watching** you?
Martin	**No, they weren't.** They **were looking** in a shop window.
Policeman	What **were they wearing**?
Martin	The woman **was wearing** a green sweatshirt.
Policeman	**Was she wearing** jeans?
Martin	**Yes, she was.** Anyway, while I **was waiting** for my money, the woman said 'Excuse me.'
Policeman	What did you do?
Martin	I looked round but she was running away. While I **wasn't looking** at the cash machine, the man took my money!

b **Practise the conversation with a partner.**

2 **Read the examples. Study the rules on page 107.**

Past continuous	
We use the past continuous for an activity in progress in the past.	
I **was waiting** for my money.	I **wasn't wearing** a sweatshirt.
They **were looking** in a window.	They **weren't watching** me.
Was she **wearing** jeans?	Yes, she **was**. No, she **wasn't**.
Were they **watching** you?	Yes, they **were**. No, they **weren't**.
What **was** she **wearing**?	What **were** they **doing**?

3a **What were these people doing when the robbery happened? Use the cues.**

1 They weren't working. They were having a break.

1 work / have a break
2 talk on a mobile / eat a hamburger
3 shop / clean windows
4 get on a bus / get in a taxi
5 come out of the bank / wait for a bus
6 read a newspaper / buy a newspaper

b **Ask and answer about the pictures.**

A *Were the men working?*

B *No, they weren't. They were having a break.*

4a Your life **What were you doing at these times?**

1 I was lying in bed at seven o'clock this morning.

1 at seven o'clock this morning
2 at 9.30 last night
3 at 10.30 last Saturday morning
4 an hour ago
5 at 4.30 yesterday afternoon
6 at two o'clock last Sunday afternoon

b **Ask and answer.**

A *What were you doing at seven o'clock this morning?*

B *I was lying in bed.*

✓ **Now I can ...** *talk about activities in progress in the past.*

1a `23.1` **Read and listen to the story. Who are these people?**
– Beatrix   – Fiona   – Daniel   – Michael

b Which of the people are in the pictures?

THE GARDENER

My name's Beatrix and I'm from the USA. Four years ago we were on holiday in Ireland. We were staying at a beautiful old hotel.

On the first afternoon, my husband and our two children were playing tennis, but I was having a rest in our room. I ordered some tea from the restaurant. While I was waiting for the tea, I looked out of the window. I saw an old man in the middle of the garden. He was wearing a jacket and a black hat and he was digging.

While I was watching the man, someone knocked at the door. I opened the door and Daniel, a young waiter, came in with my tea. I looked out of the window again but the old man wasn't there.

'The garden's beautiful,' I said. 'How many gardeners have you got here?'

'Just one,' said Daniel, 'But she isn't here today.'

'*She*?' I said. 'But I was watching your gardener when you knocked at the door. He was an old man.'

'No,' he said. 'Our gardener's a young woman. Her name's Fiona.'

Later, we were going to the restaurant for dinner. We were walking along a corridor. There were some old photographs on the walls. When I saw one of the photographs, I stopped. It was the old man in the garden.

Just then Daniel came out of the restaurant. While he was walking past us, I pointed to the photograph and I said, 'That's the old man in the garden. He was wearing that jacket and hat.'

'That's impossible!' said Daniel. 'That's Michael. He was the gardener here, but he died fifty years ago!'

2a Read the text again. Answer the questions.
1 Where is Beatrix from?
2 Where is the hotel?
3 Who was Beatrix on holiday with?
4 Where was her husband that afternoon?
5 Where was the old man?
6 What was he doing?
7 Why did Daniel go to the hotel room?
8 What did they see later?

b Who says these things in the text? Why?
'She?'
'That's impossible!'

> ### Language note
> ### Past continuous and past simple
>
> While I **was waiting**, I **saw** a man.
> I was waiting (past continuous)
> ---------------------------------→
>   I saw a man (past simple)
>
> When I **saw** the photograph, I **stopped**.
> -------------------------------------→
> I saw the photograph   I stopped
> (past simple)   (past simple)

3 Put the verbs into the correct tense.
1 While Beatrix *was having* a rest, she *decided* to order some tea. (have / decide)
2 She _____ the tea and then she _____ the phone down. (order / put)
3 While she _____ the tea, she _____ someone in the garden. (wait for / see)
4 While she _____ the old man, Daniel _____ with the tea. (watch / arrive)
5 While Beatrix and her family _____ to dinner, they _____ some old photographs. (go / see)
6 When Beatrix _____ the photo of the old man, she _____. (see / stop)

4 Writing Write a story about an unusual event. Answer the questions.
1 Where and when did it happen?
2 What were you doing?
3 What happened?
4 What happened next?
5 What was the result?

> ☑ **Now I can ...**
> *understand and write a short story.*

1 24.1 **Listen and repeat.**

1 traffic lights   2 a roundabout   3 a junction

2a Read the emails.

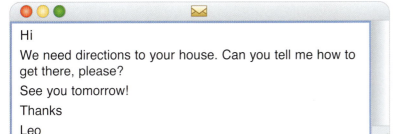

Hi

We need directions to your house. Can you tell me how to get there, please?

See you tomorrow!

Thanks

Leo

Hi Leo

Here are the directions to our house …

When you leave the motorway, turn ¹*right/left*. Go ²*up/along* that road for about a kilometre. Look for a petrol station on the ³*right/corner*. At the next traffic lights turn ⁴*right/left*. There's a post office on the ⁵*corner/left*. Go ⁶*up/down* the hill. At the ⁷*top/bottom* of the hill there's a big roundabout. Go ⁸*round/over* the roundabout and then ⁹*right/straight on*. Go ¹⁰*past/through* a shopping centre on the left-hand side. After about two hundred metres you go ¹¹*over/under* a bridge. Then at the next junction turn ¹²*right/left* into East Road. Then take the ¹³*first/second* turning on the left, and our house is ¹⁴*at the end/in the middle* of that street on the right-hand side.

Looking forward to seeing you!

Mona

b 24.2 **Listen. Choose the correct words.**

3 You're in the car with Leo. Tell him what to do next.

  1 Turn left and go along that road for about a kilometre.

  1 You're leaving the motorway.
  2 You're going past the petrol station.
  3 You're coming to the roundabout.
  4 You're going past the shopping centre.
  5 You're turning into East Road.

4 Complete the expressions.

> **Useful expressions** Giving directions
>
> Can you tell me _____ to get there?
> Here are the _____ to our house.
> Go along that road _____ about a km.
> Look _____ a petrol station.
> There's a post office _____ the corner.
> _____ about two hundred metres …
> Take _____ second turning on the left.

5 Work with a partner. Make conversations to get from your language school to:
  – the post office
  – the (bus) station
  – the nearest cash machine
  – the cinema.
  A *Can you tell me how to get to the post office, please?*
  B *Yes. Go …*

6 Your life **Write an email with directions to your home.**

Hi there
Here are the directions to our house.
When you leave the motorway/come out of the station …

English in the world
Speed limits

In Britain and the USA, speeds are given in miles per hour (mph).
(1 mile = 1.6 kilometres)
British speed limits are:

(70) top speed limit on motorways.

(60) top speed limit on other roads.

(30) the normal speed limit in towns.

In the USA, the top speed limit is usually 55 mph, but it goes up to 65 mph on some Interstate Highways.

Compare this with your country.

> ✓ Now I can …
> *ask for and give directions.*

1 **25.1** Listen and repeat.

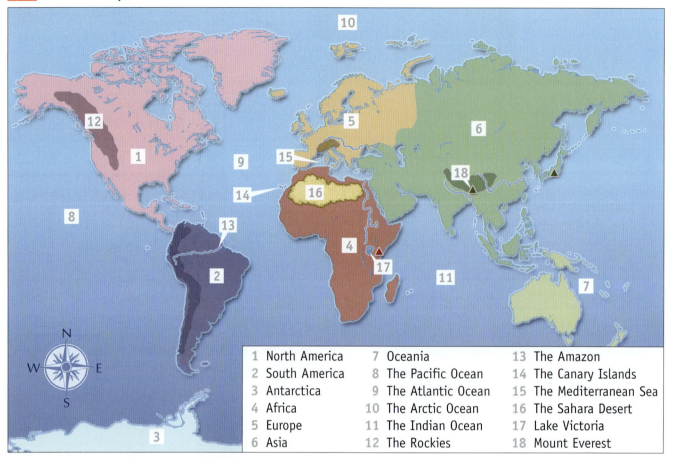

1	North America	7	Oceania	13	The Amazon
2	South America	8	The Pacific Ocean	14	The Canary Islands
3	Antarctica	9	The Atlantic Ocean	15	The Mediterranean Sea
4	Africa	10	The Arctic Ocean	16	The Sahara Desert
5	Europe	11	The Indian Ocean	17	Lake Victoria
6	Asia	12	The Rockies	18	Mount Everest

Language note Articles with geographical names

Egypt is in Africa.
NOT ~~The Egypt is in the Africa.~~

The Atlantic (Ocean)	BUT	Lake Victoria
The Sahara (Desert)		Mount Everest

2 Which continent are the places in?

1 The Rockies are in North America.

1	The Rockies	5	New Zealand
2	France	6	Lake Victoria
3	The River Amazon	7	The South Pole
4	Mount Everest	8	Canada

3a **25.2** Listen. Match the people with the places.

1	Jules and Lidia sailed		North America.
2	Pedro flew	across	Europe.
3	Timo and Selma cycled		Africa.
4	Akane ran		the Pacific.

b Listen again. Where did they start and finish?

4 **Your life** Which places in the world do you want to visit? Why? Discuss your ideas with a partner.

Pronunciation
Word stress 3

1 **25.3** Listen. Is the stress on the first or the second syllable?

1	● Africa	6	The Pacific
2	● The Sahara	7	Antarctica
3	America	8	Europe
4	The Amazon	9	Asia
5	The Rockies	10	The Atlantic

2 **25.4** Listen, check, and repeat.

3 Listen again. Underline the syllables with the schwa /ə/ sound.

✓ **Now I can ...**
name different parts of the world.

1a **26.1** Read and listen.

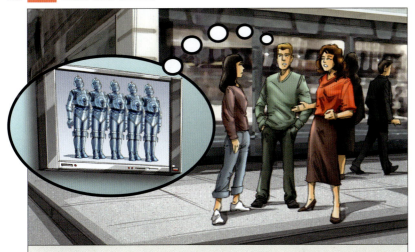

Lucy Guess what! Jordan**'s going to** be on TV on Friday.

Sarah Really? **Are you going to** be on the news?

Jordan **No, I'm not.** Don't you remember? I had a part in a TV advert in April.

Sarah Oh, yes. I remember. What time **is it going to** be on?

Lucy About 9.30. We**'re going to** watch it at my place. Do you and Peter want to join us for a drink first?

Sarah Thanks. Great. Oh, I can't believe it. I**'m going to** see Jordan on TV.

Jordan Well, you **aren't going to** see <u>me</u> exactly. … I'm one of the robots!

b Work in a group of three. Practise the conversation.

2 Read the examples. Study the rules on page 107.

going to: statements	
We use *going to* for:	
intentions	We**'re going to** watch it at my place.
a definite future	Jordan**'s going to** be on TV on Friday.
I**'m going to** watch a film.	I**'m not going to** watch a film.
He**'s going to** be on TV.	He **isn't going to** be on TV.
We**'re going to** have a party.	We **aren't going to** have a party.

3 Correct these statements.

1 Jordan isn't going to be in a film. He's going to be in a TV advert.

1 Jordan's going to be in a film.
2 They're going to watch it at Jordan's place.
3 It's going to be on at eight o'clock.
4 They're going to have a party first.
5 Jordan's going to be the star.

4 Read the examples. Study the rules on page 108.

going to: questions and short answers		
Is he **going to** be on the news?	Yes, he **is**.	No, he **isn't**.
Are you **going to** watch it?	Yes, I **am**.	No, I**'m not**.
Where **are** you **going to** watch it?		

5a **26.2** Listen. What are the people going to do this evening? Match the names with the activities.

1 Andy _*e*_
2 Shana and Omar __
3 Rosie __
4 Bruno and Martina __
5 Bradley __
6 Emma and Roy __

a have a meal with friends
b play tennis
c send some emails
d go to the gym
e have an early night
f watch a DVD

b Ask and answer about the people.

A *Is Andy going to play tennis?*
B *No, he isn't. He's going to have an early night.*

6a Speaking Are you going to do these things this evening?

I'm going to watch TV.
OR *I'm not going to watch TV.*

1 watch TV
2 go out
3 listen to some music
4 use the computer
5 do some work
6 do some exercise
7 cook dinner
8 read something

b Work with a partner. Ask and answer. Try to find some more information.

A *Are you going to watch TV?*
B *Yes, I am.*
A *What are you going to watch?*

✓ **Now I can …**
talk about intentions and future events.

1 Look at the picture. Answer the questions.

1 Who are the two people?
2 Where are they from?
3 What are they going to do?

With me this morning are Rachel Morgan from Wales and Stefan Popko from Poland. In October they're going to take part in the Global Challenge race.

2 [27.1] Listen. Choose the correct endings.

1 They're going to travel in
  a a yacht.
  b a small boat.
  c a speedboat.
2 They're going to sail
  a to every continent in the world.
  b from the Arctic to the Antarctic.
  c round the world.
3 The race is unusual because they're going to travel
  a from north to south.
  b from west to east.
  c from east to west.
4 The people in the race are from
  a all over the world.
  b several European countries.
  c the UK and Poland.
5 They're going to do the race because
  a they want to break the record.
  b they want to.
  c they want to test a new yacht.

3 Listen again. What do these numbers refer to?

They're going to travel over 56,000 kilometres.

56,000   150   12   18   22   1

Language note Large numbers

We use a comma to separate large numbers.
56,000 kilometres

We say:
fifty-six **thousand** kilometres
NOT ~~fifty-six thousands of kilometres~~.

4 Listen again. Draw the route they are going to take.

START

5 Writing Complete the summary of Rachel and Stefan's journey.

In October, ¹_____ and ²_____ are going to take part in the ³_____. Rachel is from ⁴_____ and Stefan ⁵_____. They're going to sail ⁶_____ in a ⁷_____. People normally travel ⁸_____ to ⁹_____ because the wind ¹⁰_____, but Rachel and Stefan are going to travel ¹¹_____. They're going to travel ¹²_____ kms and it's going to take ¹³_____. There are going to be ¹⁴_____ yachts in the race with ¹⁵_____ people on each yacht. The people are going to be from ¹⁶_____. Each yacht is ¹⁷_____ long and the people can only take ¹⁸_____.

English in the world
Races

These are some famous races in Britain.

1 Every year, about 30,000 people take part in the London Marathon.
2 There is a boat race between Oxford and Cambridge universities on the River Thames every year.
3 In November, the London-to-Brighton rally is for vintage cars.

What famous races are there in your country?

✓ **Now I can ...**
write about a future trip.

1 Look back at Episodes 2 and 3. What happened?

2 `28.1` Read and listen to the story. Why is Sarah happy? Is Peter happy too?

3 Are the statements true (T) or false (F)?

1 Peter and Sarah are going to get married in June.
2 Sarah's family lives in Singapore.
3 Peter's parents live in Australia.
4 Peter doesn't want to get married.
5 Peter's company sold its old offices.
6 Starlight Properties bought the building.
7 They want to open a supermarket there.
8 The new café is going to be next to The Coffee Shop.

4a Complete the expressions.

Everyday expressions
Expressing doubt
We don't k____w yet.
We aren't s____e.
M____be ...
Yes, p____y.

b Work with a partner. Read the questions. Use the expressions above to give appropriate answers.

A *Where are Sarah and Peter going to get married?*

B *We don't know yet.*

1 Where are Sarah and Peter going to get married?
2 Are they going to live in Singapore?
3 Are Lucy and Jordan going to get married?
4 Are Starlight Properties going to open an Internet café?
5 Is Peter going to tell Ryan and Cindy?
6 What are Ryan and Cindy going to do?

5 Language check. <u>Underline</u> examples of *going to* in the story.

6 Work with a partner. Practise the story.

Sarah	I've got some news. Peter and I are going to get married!
Lucy	Oh, congratulations! When's the wedding?
Sarah	We don't know yet. It's going to be complicated, because my family's in Singapore and Peter's parents live in the USA.
Lucy	Yes, I see the problem. Where are you going to live?
Sarah	We aren't sure. Maybe in Singapore.
Lucy	Well, it's wonderful news. I bet Peter's happy!

Jordan	Congratulations, Peter.
Peter	What? Oh, yes. Thanks.
Jordan	You don't sound very happy.
Peter	About getting married? Oh, no. That's great.
Jordan	So, what's wrong?
Peter	You know that we sold our offices a few weeks ago.
Jordan	Yes, to Starlight Properties. We fix their computers, you know.
Peter	Really? Well, anyway, it seems they aren't going to use the building for offices.
Jordan	Oh? What are they going to do, then?
Peter	People say that they're going to open a big Internet café.

What?!

Yes, probably. Right next door to The Coffee Shop!

Now I can ... *express doubt.*

1 29.1 **Listen and repeat.**

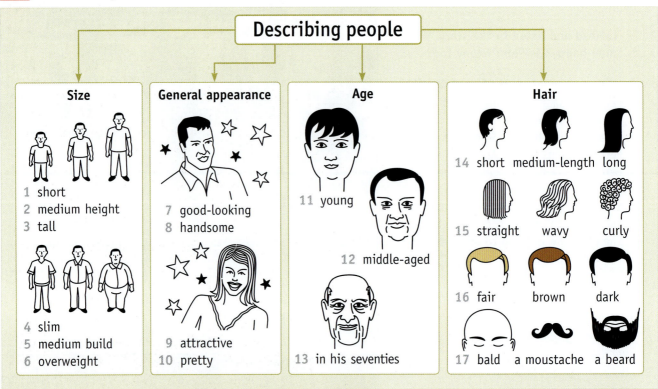

Describing people

Size
1 short
2 medium height
3 tall
4 slim
5 medium build
6 overweight

General appearance
7 good-looking
8 handsome
9 attractive
10 pretty

Age
11 young
12 middle-aged
13 in his seventies

Hair
14 short   medium-length   long
15 straight   wavy   curly
16 fair   brown   dark
17 bald   a moustache   a beard

Language note **Descriptions**

1 We ask: What does he/she look like? How tall is he/she?

2 We often use modifiers in descriptions:
very tall
quite tall
fairly tall
not very tall

3 We normally use:
attractive, pretty and beautiful for women
good-looking and handsome for men.

2a 29.2 **Listen. Which words do the people use? Underline the correct words.**

1 Imran's new boss:
 – overweight / <u>slim</u>
 – tall / short
 – in her thirties / middle-aged
 – medium-length / long hair
 – straight / wavy hair
 – dark / blonde hair
 – not very attractive / pretty

2 The police suspect:
 – middle-aged / young
 – tall / medium height
 – slim / overweight
 – straight / curly hair
 – fair / black hair
 – brown / blue eyes
 – a moustache / a beard

b Listen again. What modifiers do the people use?
She's quite slim.

---

3 **Speaking** **Describe these people to a partner. Can he/she guess who it is?**
 – someone in your class
 – a film star
 – a famous sportsperson
 – a character from the *That's Life!* story

He's in his thirties. He's tall and quite slim. He's good-looking. He's got short, dark hair and blue eyes. He's also got a beard.

4 Your life **Write a description of yourself.**

English in the world
Tactful language

When we describe people, we normally try to be tactful and polite.

We don't say:	We say:
thin →	very slim
fat →	a bit overweight
ugly →	not very good-looking
old →	in his (seventies), etc.

Compare this with your language.

✓ **Now I can ...**
describe a person's appearance.

1 30.1 **Read and listen.**

You're a **good** dancer and you danced **well**. But you chose a **bad** song and you sang it **badly**. It sounded **terrible**. So I can only give you three out of ten.

That meal was **perfect**. The wine was **excellent** and you cooked everything **perfectly**. It looked **good** and it tasted **delicious**. Ten out of ten.

Can't you forget your job when we go out, dear?

2 **Read the examples. Study the rules on page 108.**

Adjectives and adverbs

1 An adjective describes a noun:
You chose a **bad** song.
    ↑   ↑
adjective noun

An adverb describes a verb:
You sang **badly**.
  ↑   ↑
verb   adverb

2 Adjectives	quick	nice	easy	good	fast
Adverbs	quickly	nicely	easily	well	fast

3 You danced well. NOT ~~You well danced~~.
You cooked everything perfectly.
NOT ~~You cooked perfectly everything~~.

3 30.2 **Drill. Listen. Say the sentence.**
1 She's a good driver.
  She drives well.

4 **Put the words in the correct order.**
1 You're a great dancer.

1 great a dancer you're
2 very he well cooks
3 guitar you the badly play
4 a meal it delicious was
5 the sang perfectly she song
6 beautifully he piano the plays
7 song a good chose you
8 waiter he's excellent an

5a Choose the correct word.
1 Are you a *good / well* cook?
2 Do you drive *careful / carefully*?
3 Do you often sleep *bad / badly*?
4 Are you a *nice / nicely* person?
5 Do you wake up *easy / easily*?
6 Do you walk *quick / quickly*?

b Ask your partner the questions.

Language note Verb + adjective

We use an adjective after these verbs:
be, look, taste, sound.
It **sounded terrible**.
NOT ~~It sounded terribly~~.
It **looked good**. NOT ~~It looked well~~.

6a Think of a thing, person, or place for these descriptions.
1 I think this book looks interesting.

1 looks interesting
2 looks dangerous
3 tastes delicious
4 tastes awful
5 sounds beautiful
6 sounds terrible
7 is easy
8 is boring

b Compare your ideas with a partner.

7 Your life **Write six sentences about yourself. Use these words.**
good   well   bad   badly   fast   slowly

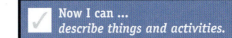

Now I can ...
describe things and activities.

1 `31.1` **Listen and repeat.**

1 shy   2 confident

3 generous

4 selfish

5 hard-working   6 lazy

7 quiet

8 noisy

2a **Read the questionnaire. Work with a partner. Ask the questions.**

A *Do you like getting up late?*
B *Yes, I do. / I don't mind it. / No, I don't.*

What kind of person are *you?*

Do you like these things?

	I like it	I don't mind it	I don't like it
1 getting up late	☐	☐	☐
2 writing emails	☐	☐	☐
3 eating new kinds of food	☐	☐	☐
4 going to parties	☐	☐	☐
5 travelling	☐	☐	☐
6 talking on the phone	☐	☐	☐
7 shopping	☐	☐	☐
8 meeting new people	☐	☐	☐
9 working with other people	☐	☐	☐
10 dancing	☐	☐	☐

Score: **3** for every 'I like it'.
1 for every 'I don't mind it'.
0 for every 'I don't like it'.

b **Calculate your score.**

3a `31.2` **Read and listen. Write the missing words from exercise 1.**

21–30: You love talking and having a good time. You look ¹*confident*, but you hate being alone. You're usually ²_____. You don't like working at a desk and you're sometimes a bit ³_____. You do things quickly and you don't always finish jobs completely.

11–20: You like talking to people, but you don't mind being alone. You like meeting people and going to parties, but you often leave early. You're ⁴_____. You can do things easily and you work fast, so you prefer working alone. You can sometimes be a bit ⁵_____.

0–10: You're quite ⁶_____ and you like a ⁷_____ life. You prefer being alone or with a very good friend. You don't like talking to people and you hate ⁸_____ people. You love reading books. You work hard, but you do things slowly and carefully.

b **What kind of person are you? Do you agree with the result?**

Language note
Expressing likes and dislikes

☺ I love
   I like   talk**ing**.
   I prefer   be**ing** alone.
   I don't mind   danc**ing**.
   I hate   shop**ping**.
☹ I can't stand

4a **Writing** **Write a paragraph about your likes and dislikes. Use this model.**

I love ... . I like ... , too, but I prefer ... . I don't mind ... , but I hate ... , and I can't stand ... .

b **Compare your ideas with a partner.**

A *I love cooking. Do you?*
B *I don't mind it. / No, I can't stand it.*

Now I can ...
talk about personality, likes, and dislikes.

1a 32.1 Read and listen.

A Can I help you?

B Yes. How much are those watches, please?

A The gold ones?

B No, the silver ones.

A The small one is €65 and the large one is €80.

B Can I have a look at the large one, please?

A Certainly. Here you are.

B Thank you. Hmm, it's a bit big.

A Would you like to see the other one?

B Yes, please. Yes. I think I prefer this one. I'll take it. How much is it again?

A €65. Anything else?

B No, thank you.

A That's €65, then, please.

b Work with a partner. Practise the conversation.

Language note *one / ones*

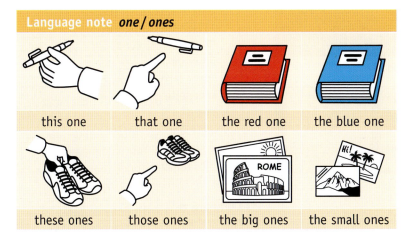

| this one | that one | the red one | the blue one |
| these ones | those ones | the big ones | the small ones |

2 Ask and answer. Use the cues.

1 **A** *Do you like this mobile?*

  B *I prefer the other one.*

1 this mobile / other
2 those earrings / gold
3 these bags / those
4 that camera / small
5 this watch / black
6 these shoes / brown
7 this umbrella / large
8 these sunglasses / other

3 Complete the expressions.

Everyday expressions **In a shop**

Can I _____ you?
How _____ are those watches?
Can I have a _____ at that one, please?
Would you _____ to see the other one?
I think I _____ this one.
I'll take _____ .

4 32.2 Listen to two conversations.

1 How much is each thing?
2 Which things do the people buy?

5 Work with a partner. Use the things in exercise 4. Make the conversations.

Pronunciation
Sentence stress

32.3 **Listen and repeat. Use the same rhythm.**

1 How much are those bags
  How much are those bags over there?

2 Can we have a look
  Can we have a look at the large one?

3 Would you like to see
  Would you like to see the other one?

✓ **Now I can ...**
describe things in a shop.

1 `33.1` **Listen and repeat.**

1 a sports programme

2 a documentary

3 a soap (opera)

4 a sitcom

5 the news

6 the weather forecast

7 a police drama

8 a hospital drama

9 a film / movie

10 a cartoon

11 a reality TV show

12 a chat show

13 a game show

14 a TV advert

2 **Give some examples of programmes from your country.**

Language note **Word building 2**

This programme is about music.
It's **a music programme**.
This drama is about a hospital.
It's **a hospital drama**.

3 `33.2` **Listen. What kinds of programme do the people like and dislike? Complete the table.**

	✓	✗
Bob	*the news, the ...*	
Anna		
Julie		
Ivor		

4 **Your life** **Work with a partner. Talk about the programmes that you like/dislike. Use these questions.**

1 Do you watch a lot of TV?
2 What kinds of programme do you like?
3 What programmes don't you like?
4 Do you ever watch ... ?
5 What's your favourite programme?
6 Who's your favourite newsreader?
7 What did you watch last night?
8 What are you going to watch tonight?

English in the world
TV channels

In Britain there are three kinds of TV channels:

1 The BBC (British Broadcasting Corporation) gets its money from the government. Everybody with a TV pays an annual licence fee.
2 Commercial TV channels like ITV and Channel 4 get most of their money from adverts.
3 Cable and satellite TV have hundreds of channels. You pay a monthly subscription to get these channels. Most of them have adverts, too.

Compare this with your country.

✓ **Now I can ...**
talk about TV programmes.

1 `34.1` **Read and listen.**

Lucy Oh, it's the lottery. I must check my ticket. ... No, nothing this week.

Peter Have you ever won anything on the lottery?

Lucy Yes, I have. I've had a few small prizes. Jordan's been very lucky.

Peter Really?

Lucy Yes. He hasn't won millions of pounds, but he's received two big prizes of about £1,000 each.

Peter Wow! That's good.

Lucy What about you? Have you ever won anything on the lottery?

Peter No, I haven't.

Lucy Oh, dear. Well, you've been very unlucky.

Peter No, not really. I've never bought a ticket.

2 **Read the examples. Study the rules on page 109.**

Present perfect
1 We use the present perfect for experiences in our lives up to now. We are not interested in <u>when</u> these things happened. I've had a few small prizes. (up to now) He's been very lucky.   (up to now)
2 I've received a prize.   I haven't received a prize. He's won the lottery.   He hasn't won the lottery.

3 **Have you ever done these things?**

1 I've been on TV. OR *I haven't been on TV or the radio.*

1 be on TV or the radio
2 meet a famous person
3 fall in love
4 miss a plane
5 save someone's life
6 steal anything
7 write a poem
8 forget someone's name

Language note **Experiences**
When we talk about experiences, we often use *ever* and *never*. Have you **ever** won anything? (in your life) I've **never** bought a ticket. (in my life)
When we're talking about experiences, we use *have / has been* as the present perfect of *go*. She's **been** to China.   She's **gone** to China. (She's back now)   (She's in China now)
I've never been to China. NOT ~~I've never gone to China.~~

4 **Write six sentences.**

– three things that you have done
– three things that you have never done

I've been to the USA.

I've never ridden a horse.

5 **Read the examples. Study the rules on page 109.**

Present perfect: Questions and short answers	
Have you ever **missed** a plane?	Yes, I **have**. No, I **haven't**.
Has she ever **been** on TV?	Yes, she **has**. No, she **hasn't**.

6 `34.2` **Drill. Listen. Make the questions.**

1 win a prize
   Have you ever won a prize?
2 go to Africa
   Have you ever been to Africa?

7a `Your life` **Work with a partner. Ask questions. Use the cues in exercise 3.**

A *Have you ever been on TV?*
B *Yes, I have. / No, I haven't.*

b **Work with a new partner. Ask about your first partners.**

A *Has Carla ever been on TV?*
B *Yes, she has. / No, she hasn't.*

✓	Now I can ... *talk about past experiences.*

1 Read the news stories.

THE NEWS

TODAY'S HEADLINES

1 The heads of government of the ~~G8~~ *EU* countries have arrived in ~~Berlin~~ *Budapest* for their latest meeting.

2 Thieves have stolen money and a large number of diamonds from a jewellery shop in Paris.

3 A tropical storm has hit the coast of North America. Strong winds have destroyed several buildings. More than a hundred people have lost their lives.

4 Four people have died in a fire at a house in Glasgow.

5 There has been a serious accident on the M5 motorway. A lorry has crashed into a bridge. The police have closed the motorway in both directions between junctions 5 and 8.

6 The comedy programme, *The Box*, has won the Independent award for the best TV programme of the year.

7 Alan Jones, star of the TV soap opera *The Avenue*, has married the programme's producer, Rajni Sekar.

2 | 35.1 | **Listen. There are two mistakes in each story. Underline the parts that are incorrect.**

3a Correct the stories. Read them to your partner.

b Listen again and check.

Language note	Present perfect with present result
We use the present perfect for a past action with a result in the present. We don't know <u>when</u> the action happened.	
Past action	**Present result**
The police **have closed** the motorway.	You can't use the motorway now.
Thieves **have stolen** some diamonds.	The diamonds aren't in the bank now.

4 Change the newspaper headlines into full sentences.

1 *Some thieves have stolen a famous painting.*

1 **Thieves steal famous painting**

2 **POLICE CLOSE BRIDGE**

3 **STORM HITS WEST COAST**

4 **Fire destroys cinema**

5 **LOCAL TEAM WINS CUP**

6 **Lorry kills dog**

7 **FILM STAR VISITS SCHOOL**

8 **Prime Minister flies to Tokyo**

5a Writing What's in the news today? Write the headlines for three news stories.

b Work in a group. Present your headlines as a news programme.

Pronunciation
The letter *o*

1 | 35.2 | **Listen and repeat.**

/ɒ/	/ɔː/	/əʊ/	/ʌ/
sh**o**p	st**o**rm	st**o**len	m**o**ney

2a Put these words in the correct column above.

more   won   comedy   both   sport   programme   government   tropical   closed   short   strong   forecast   love   lorry   broken   some

b | 35.3 | **Listen and check.**

c Listen again and repeat.

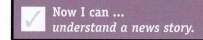

Now I can ...
understand a news story.

1 Look back at Episodes 3 and 4. What happened?

2 36.1 Read and listen to the story. What is 'the news'?

3 Choose the correct words.

1 The party is at *Lucy's / Jordan's* place.
2 The actors and actresses are near the *kitchen / bedroom*.
3 Jordan met them when he was making *an advert / a film*.
4 Anna Harlow is wearing a *black / red* dress.
5 She arrived with *Lucy / Russell*.
6 Russell met Anna *inside / outside* The Coffee Shop.
7 Ryan looks *happy / unhappy*.
8 Ryan and Cindy *know / don't know* about the new café.

4a Complete the expressions.

> **Everyday expressions**
> **Expressing opinions 1**
>
> **Making statements**
> I th____k ...
> I bel____ve ...
>
> **Responding**
> (Yes,) I think s____.
> (No,) I don't think s____.

b Work with a partner. Use the expressions above. Express your opinions about these things:

A *Reality TV shows are awful!*
B *Yes, I think so, too.*
OR
B *No, I don't think so.*

– reality TV shows
– today's news
– the government
– mobile phones
– football
– the news about the café

5 Language check. <u>Underline</u> examples of the present perfect in the story.

6 Work in a group. Practise the story.

1 *Jordan's having a party in his flat. Sarah and Peter have just arrived.*

Sarah Who are those people near the kitchen? They look very stylish.
Jordan They're actors and actresses.
Peter Did you meet them when you were making that TV advert?
Jordan Yes, that's right.
Sarah Anybody famous?
Jordan No, I don't think so.
Peter I think I've seen that blonde woman in the red dress before.
Jordan She isn't an actress. She arrived with Russell.
Sarah Oh, is that Anna Harlow?
Jordan Yes, I think so.
Peter Who's Anna Harlow?
Sarah Russell met her outside The Coffee Shop. I believe she wants to open a shop round here.

Peter Hi, Lucy. Are Cindy and Ryan here?
Lucy Yes, they are.
Sarah Ryan's over there, but I can't see Cindy.
Peter Perhaps she's on the balcony.
Lucy Yes, maybe.
Sarah Ryan looks happy.
Peter Well, he probably hasn't heard about the new café. We haven't said anything.
Lucy Well, he and Cindy aren't going to like it when they hear the news.

What news is that, Lucy?

> ✓ Now I can ...
> *give and respond to opinions.*

1 `37.1` **Listen and repeat.**

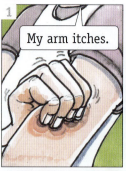

1 My arm itches.

2 My thumb's painful.

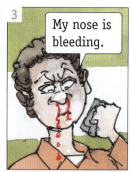

3 My nose is bleeding.

4 My elbow's swollen.

5 I feel sick.

6 I've got a rash.

7 I've got an infection.

8 I've got a temperature.

9 I've got a cold.

10 I've got flu.

11 I've hurt my knee.

12 I've burnt my hand.

13 I've cut my finger.

14 I've bruised my leg.

15 I've sprained my ankle.

2 **What other words or expressions do you know for ... ?**
- parts of the body
- illnesses

Language note **Possessive adjectives**
My head itches.   I've hurt **my** ankle.   **His** finger is swollen.   She's cut **her** thumb.   I've got a bruise on **my** arm.   You've got a rash on **your** hand.

3 **Say what's wrong. Use the cues.**

1 *She's bruised her knee. Her knee's painful.*

1 She / bruise / knee. Knee / painful
2 I / rash / leg. Leg / itch
3 He / sprain / wrist. Wrist / swollen
4 You / cut / finger. Finger / bleeding
5 She / burn / hand. Hand / painful
6 I / bruise / thumb. Thumb / swollen

4 `37.2` **Listen. Write the problem next to the correct remedy.**

Problem	Remedy
	a ice
	b plasters
	c cream
a headache	d painkillers
	e cold water
	f tissues

5 **Work with a partner. Make the conversations. Use the table in exercise 4.**

A *What's the matter?*
B *I've got a headache.*
A *Oh dear. Here, I've got some painkillers.*
B *Thanks.*

✓	Now I can ... *talk about some health problems.*

1a `38.1` **Read and listen.**

Peter Hello, Ryan. What **have you done** to your foot?
Ryan I**'ve bruised** my big toe.
Peter How **did you do** that?
Ryan I **dropped** a laptop on it this morning.
Peter Really? Ha, ha!

Don't laugh. It was your laptop. You **left** it here yesterday.

b **Practise the conversation with a partner.**

2 **Read the examples. Study the rules on page 109.**

> ### Present perfect and past simple
>
> **1 We use the present perfect for:**
>
> – **a past action with a result in the present. We're interested in the result, NOT the action:**
>   I**'ve bruised** my big toe. ----→ (My toe hurts now.)
>
> – **experiences up to the present:**
>   I**'ve never had** flu. ----→ (up to now)
>
> **2 We use the past simple for:**
>
> – **a completed action in the past. We're interested in the action itself:**
>   I **dropped** a laptop on it.
>
> – **the actual time of the event:**
>   I **broke** my arm last year. NOT ~~I've broken my arm last year.~~

3 `38.2` **Drill. Listen. Say the sentence.**

1 I've broken your laptop.
  I broke it yesterday.

2 I've hurt my foot.
  I hurt it yesterday.

4a `38.3` **Listen to three conversations. Answer these questions each time.**

1 What has he / she done?
2 How did he / she do it?
3 When did it happen?

b **Work with a partner. Make the conversations. Use your answers to the questions. Follow the pattern.**

A *What have you done to your elbow?*
B *I've sprained it.*
A *How did you do that?*
B *I fell downstairs.*
A *Really? When did it happen?*
B *On Thursday.*

5a **Speaking Tick ✓ the things you have done.**

– had flu
– broken a bone
– lost some money
– fallen off a bike
– dropped something on your foot
– seen an accident
– sprained your ankle
– left something on a bus or train.

b **Ask and answer with a partner. Try to find some more information. Use these questions:**

How did you … ?
When did you … ?
Why were you … ?
What did you … ?
Did you … ?
Were you … ?

A *Have you ever had flu?*
B *Yes, I have.*
A *When did you have it?*
B *When I was fifteen.*
A *Did you stay in bed?*

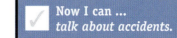

Now I can …
talk about accidents.

1 39.1 **Read and listen to the text.**

Advice for travellers

It's holiday time again. Here's some advice to make your holiday easier.

6 Six weeks before you go

Have you had any necessary vaccinations? If not, see your doctor. Have you checked your passport? Is it still valid? If not, get a new one now.

🧳 Packing

1 Don't forget to take:
- medical items:
  – painkillers
  – plasters
  – something for insect bites
  – sunscreen
- toiletry items:
  – toothbrushes
  – toothpaste
  – a hairbrush
- glasses and sunglasses
- your mobile phone and charger
- keys for the luggage

2 Don't put these things in your suitcase:
- any personal medicine (tablets, etc.)
- your passport and tickets
- money or credit cards
- jewellery
- a camera or camcorder
- a child's favourite toy

3 Don't put these things in your hand luggage:
- scissors
- knives
- more than one book or magazine. (They're heavy.)

✈ On the plane

1 Wear comfortable clothes.
2 Avoid alcohol and coffee. They cause dehydration. It's best to drink plenty of water.
3 Don't eat a lot.
4 Don't stay in your seat for a long time. Try to take some exercise. It's a good idea to get up and walk every hour. When you are sitting down, move your legs and feet.

2 Which of these things does the text mention? What does it say about each item?

3 What does the text say about ... ?
- books
- water
- exercise

Language note **Giving advice**
Wear (comfortable clothes).
Don't (eat a lot).
Avoid (alcohol).
Don't forget to ...
It's a good idea to ...
It's best to ...
Try to ...

4 Your life **What do you always take when you travel? Name six things.**

5 Writing **Write some advice for travellers to your country. Follow the pattern. Use the expressions in the Language note.**

> *Here's some advice for people coming to _____.*
>
> ***Things to pack***
> *1 It's a good idea to ...*
> *2 Don't forget to ...*
>
> ***When you're here***
> *1 Try to ...*
> *2 It's best to ...*
> *3 Wear ...*
> *4 Don't eat ...*

Pronunciation
Plural -es endings

1 39.2 **Listen and repeat.**

/z/	/ɪz/
tissues	toothbrushes

2a Put these words in the correct column above.

sunglasses   knives   magazines   boxes
sandwiches   bottles   phones   offices
shoes   purses   exercises   clothes

b 39.3 **Listen, check, and repeat.**

Now I can ...
understand and give advice.

1 `40.1` **Read and listen.**

Doctor Good morning. What seems to be the problem?

Patient I've got a pain in my chest.

Doctor I see. When did it start?

Patient Oh, about three days ago.

Doctor Can I just have a look at it? Where does it hurt?

Patient Here in my chest near my left shoulder.

Doctor Can you lift your arm, please? Does that hurt?

Patient Yes, it does.

Doctor Well, I think you've pulled a muscle.

Patient Oh, that's good.

Doctor Yes, but we'd better check your heart, too. Can you make an appointment with the nurse for a check-up, please?

Patient OK.

Doctor In the meantime, don't lift anything heavy, and move your arm slowly.

Patient Yes, OK. Thank you. Goodbye.

Doctor Goodbye.

2 **Read the conversation again. Choose the correct answers.**

1 The patient has come to see the doctor, because
a his shoulder is swollen.   b he's got a pain in his chest.

2 The problem started
a yesterday.   b three days ago.

3 The doctor thinks
a he's pulled a muscle.   b he's had a heart attack.

4 The patient has to
a see the doctor again.   b see the nurse for a check-up.

5 In the meantime, he has to
a move his arm slowly.   b lift heavy things.

3 **Practise the conversation with a partner.**

4 **Complete the expressions.**

> **Everyday expressions** At the doctor's
>
> What seems to _____ the problem?
> When did it _____?
> Can I just _____ a look at it?
> Where _____ it hurt?
> We'd _____ check your heart.
> In _____ meantime, ...

5a `40.2` **Listen to two conversations. Answer the questions for each one.**

1 What's the problem?
2 When did the problem start?
3 What does the doctor think it is?
4 What is the treatment?

b **Work with a partner. Use the information from exercise 5a. Make the conversations.**

> ✓ Now I can ...
> *understand a conversation at the doctor's.*

1 41.1 Listen and repeat.

1 a saucepan

2 a frying pan

3 a bowl

4 a plate

5 boil

6 fry

7 roast

8 bake

9 grill

10 mix

11 add

12 weigh

13 peel

14 pour

15 slice

16 stir

2 41.2 Drill. Listen. Say what you've done.

1 Put some water in a saucepan.
OK. I've put some water in a saucepan.

Language note	Verbs and adjectives	
We can use the past participle of the verb as an adjective:		
verb	fry	grill
adjective	a **fried** egg	**grilled** fish

3a 41.3 Listen. What does the man order?

TODAY'S SPECIALS

grilled salmon   a baked potato
fried chicken   boiled potatoes
omelette   chips
a mixed salad
roasted vegetables
boiled vegetables

b Complete the conversation.

A Are you ready to order?
B Yes. Can I have the [1]_____, please?
A What kind of potatoes would you like – baked, boiled, or chips?
B Oh, [2]_____, please.
A And what would you like with that?
B Oh, can I have [3]_____, please?
A OK, so that's [4]_____ with [5]_____ and [6]_____.
B Thank you.

4 Speaking Work with a partner. Make new conversations. Use the menu.

English in the world
Eating

In Britain, it's polite to eat everything on your plate. It shows that you have enjoyed the meal.

In China, however, it's polite to leave some food. It shows that your hosts have given you enough food.

Compare this with your country.

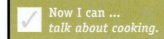
✓ Now I can ...
talk about cooking.

1a Label the things in the picture.

> bread   fruit   sugar   water   a knife   a plate
> a spoon   a bowl   a saucepan   a fork

> Today I'm going to make Summer Pudding. It's **an** easy recipe. You don't need **many** things for it and it doesn't take **much** time.

> You need **some** soft fruit. I've got some raspberries, some blueberries, and **a few** strawberries. You also need a few slices of white bread, 150 grams of sugar, and **a little** water.

b `42.1` **Read and listen.**

2 Read the examples. Study the rules on page 110.

Expressing quantity	
Countable nouns	**Uncountable nouns**
You need **a** saucepan. NOT ~~You need saucepan.~~ I've got **some raspberries**. I haven't got **any apples**.	You need **some fruit**. You don't need **any milk**.
You need **a few** things. You don't need **many** things. **How many** things do we need?	You need **a little** water. You don't need **much** water. **How much** water do we need?

3 `42.2` **Drill. Listen. Say the sentence. Use** *much/many*.

1 eggs
   You don't need many eggs.

2 salt
   You don't need much salt.

4 Work with a partner. Ask and answer. Use the cues.

– strawberries	– bottles of water
– sugar	– pieces of paper
– milk	– beef
– slices of toast	– eggs
– wine	– butter

A *How many strawberries do you want?*
B *Oh, just a few.*
A *How much sugar do you want?*
B *Oh, just a little.*

> **Language note Quantity expressions**
>
> **To talk about 'how much' of an uncountable thing, we use a quantity expression:**
>
> **a slice of** bread   **a kilo of** fruit
> **two slices of** bread   **two kilos of** fruit

5a Read the recipe. Choose the correct word.

So, we're going to make Summer Pudding. We've got ¹*a/some* nice soft fruit. First, wash the fruit and put it in ²*a/some* saucepan with ³*a/some* sugar. Add ⁴*a little/a few* water. Then cook the fruit for ⁵*a little/a few* minutes. Try the fruit and add ⁶*a little/a few* more sugar, if you need it. Now take ⁷*a little/a few* slices of white bread. Put the bread in ⁸*a/some* bowl. Pour the fruit into the bowl. Put ⁹*a little/a few* more bread on top of the fruit. Put ¹⁰*a/some* plate on top and put the bowl in the fridge for ¹¹*a little/a few* hours. Serve the Summer Pudding with ¹²*a little/a few* cream or ¹³*a/some* milk.

b `42.3` **Listen and check.**

6a Writing Tell a partner how to make a simple dish or drink, for example:

– a boiled egg	– grilled fish
– a fruit salad	– a cup of tea or coffee

b Write down the recipe. Follow the pattern.

> *This is a recipe for …*
> *You need …*
> *First you …*
> *Then you …*
> *Serve the … with …*

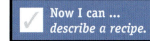

> ✓ Now I can …
> *describe a recipe.*

1 `43.1` **Read and listen to the text. Choose the correct answers.**

1 What is the basic rule of the diet?
   a You eat a little but often.
   b You don't eat anything on one day a week.
   c You only eat one meal a day.

2 When does he eat?
   a in the evening
   b every four hours
   c in the morning

Eat as much as you like

Can you eat a lot and lose weight? Callum Briggs, 43, thinks you can.

'I've always liked food. I was slim when I was young. However, when I was 40, I was very overweight and I didn't have much energy. My doctor gave me lots of information about diets and exercise, but it was very complicated. Then I read about this new diet in the newspaper. It's very simple. You eat only one meal a day – in the evening, so I don't eat breakfast or lunch. However, for dinner in the evening you can eat as much as you like.

So, a normal dinner for me is a big piece of grilled fish or a really big steak with a medium-sized bowl of pasta or a couple of baked potatoes, and a lot of vegetables or salad. I often have one or two fried eggs with that. Then I have dessert – some fruit or a big slice of apple pie with cream. After that I have some cheese with several biscuits and a couple of glasses of wine, too.

I have dinner at nine o'clock, so when I go to bed I feel very full. However, I always sleep well.

I started the diet a few months ago. It was very hard at first. I felt very hungry by midday and I wanted a biscuit or a sandwich, but it's OK now. I don't have any snacks and I just drink lots of water during the day. And it works. I've lost twenty kilos. I've got more energy, too, so I feel great.'

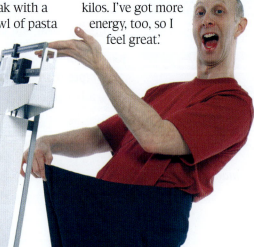

2 **Answer the questions.**

1 Why did Callum start the diet?
2 How did he learn about it?
3 What meals doesn't he eat?
4 What time does he eat dinner?
5 Does he sleep well?
6 When did he start the diet?
7 Has he lost any weight?
8 How does he feel now?

> **Language note** *but* and *however*
>
> I feel full, **but** I always sleep well.
> I feel full. **However,** I always sleep well.

3 **Join the sentences with *but* and then with *however*.**

1 I got lots of information. It was complicated.
2 I don't eat lunch. I eat a big dinner.
3 I eat a lot. I've lost a lot of weight.
4 I tried a lot of diets. They didn't work.
5 The diet was hard at first. It's OK now.
6 I only eat one meal a day. I eat as much as I like.

4 **What kinds of food and drink does Callum mention? What quantities does he eat?**

a big piece of grilled fish
lots of water

5 `Your life` **Discuss these questions.**

1 What do you think of the diet?
2 Why do you think it works?
3 Do you know any other kinds of diet?
4 Do you think diets are a good idea?
5 What do you think is a healthy diet?

> ### Pronunciation
> ## The letter *i*
>
> **1** `43.2` **Listen and repeat.**
>
> | /ɪ/ | /aɪ/ | /ɜː/ |
> | --- | --- | --- |
> | mix | slice | first |
>
> **2a** **Put the words in the correct column above.**
>
> rice   chicken   fish   white   bird   grill
> third   drink   shirt   diet   wine   girl
>
> **b** `43.3` **Listen, check, and repeat.**

> ✓ **Now I can ...**
> *talk about eating habits.*

1 Look back at Episodes 4 and 5. What happened?

2 `44.1` Read and listen to the story. Why does Russell phone Cindy?

3 Are the statements true (T) or false (F)?

1 Russell has never borrowed the car before.
2 He's gone out with Anna.
3 Russell never puts petrol in the car.
4 He hasn't found a job.
5 Ryan gave Russell his mobile.
6 Ryan has been to see the bank manager.
7 He travelled on the bus.
8 There are two parking tickets on the car.
9 Ryan takes the car.
10 The police think that Ryan has stolen the car.

4a Complete the expressions.

> **Everyday expressions**
> **Expressing annoyance**
>
> Oh, no, _____ again!
> Oh, _____ goodness' sake!
> You _____ joking!
> You can't _____ serious!
> Oh, I don't believe _____!

b Work with a partner. Respond to these events.

A *The computer isn't working.*
B *Oh no, not again.*

1 The computer isn't working.
2 The car's gone.
3 Someone's stolen the camera.
4 Those children have broken the window.
5 There's a parking ticket on the car.
6 Someone's taken my keys.
7 I'm sorry. I've lost your mobile.
8 The shop's closed today.

5 Language check. <u>Underline</u> examples of quantity expressions in the story.

6 Work in a group. Practise the story.

1 *At The Coffee Shop…*

Ryan Oh, no, not again! Has Russell taken the car?
Cindy Yes, he has. He's gone out with Anna.
Ryan Again? And he never puts any petrol in the car.
Cindy Well, he hasn't got much money.
Ryan That's because he hasn't looked for a job.
Cindy He's borrowed your mobile, too.
Ryan Oh, for goodness' sake!

2

Lucy Hello, Ryan. What are you doing in this part of town?
Ryan Hi, Lucy. I've been to see our accountant – we're having a few problems with The Coffee Shop. Oh! This is our car!
Lucy Yes, didn't you park it here?
Ryan No, I didn't. Russell borrowed it. I came on the underground.
Lucy You've got a couple of parking tickets, Ryan.
Ryan You're joking! Well, I've got my car key, so Russell can walk home.

3

Cindy What? Somebody's stolen the car? You can't be serious.
Russell Yes. I parked it near Anna's place and now it's gone.
Cindy Well, you'd better phone the police.

4

Oh, I don't believe it!

> ✓ Now I can …
> *express annoyance.*

1 `45.1` **Listen and repeat.**

1 a baker's

2 a butcher's

3 a greengrocer's

4 a chemist's

5 a department store

6 a travel agent's

7 a newsagent's

8 an estate agent's

9 a music shop

10 a sports shop

11 a furniture shop

12 a hairdresser's

13 a jewellery shop

14 a flower shop

15 a stationery shop

16 a hardware shop

2 **What other kinds of shop do you know?**

> **Language note** Word building 3
>
> This shop sells **shoes**. (Countable noun)
> It's **a shoe shop**.
> This shop sells **furniture**. (Uncountable noun)
> It's **a furniture shop**.
>
> BUT
> a clothe**s** shop   a sport**s** shop   a bookshop

3 **Work with a partner. Ask and answer.**

A *What do you buy at a greengrocer's?*
B *You buy fruit and vegetables.*
OR
A *Where do you go to buy a ring or a watch?*
B *You go to a jewellery shop.*

4 `45.2` **Listen. Where are the people?**

1 *They're at a shoe shop.*

5a `Your life` **Think about the main shopping street in your town. Write about five places that you go to.**

1 *There's a big department store. It's called Bedfords. I often go there on Saturdays.*
2 *There are two music shops. Mercury Music is next to the General Union bank and …*

b **Compare your sentences with a partner.**

> ## Pronunciation
> ### Silent letters
>
> **1** **Which letters are not pronounced? Circle them.**
>
> 1 cam(e)ra
> 2 different
> 3 interesting
> 4 restaurant
> 5 strawberry
> 6 jewellery
> 7 stationery
> 8 everything
>
> **2** `45.3` **Listen, check, and repeat.**

> ✓ **Now I can …**
> *name different kinds of shops.*

1 46.1 **Read and listen.**

The Red Dragon is a **small** restaurant. It's very **popular**, so it's usually **busy**. The food is **good**, but the chef has got a **bad** temper.

Sandy's restaurant is **smaller** than The Red Dragon, but it's **more popular**, so it's usually **busier**. The food is **better**, but the chef has got a **worse** temper.

Mount Etna is **the smallest** restaurant in the town, but it's **the most popular** so it's always **the busiest**. It's got **the best** food. Unfortunately, the chef has got **the worst** temper.

2 **Read the examples. Study the rules on page 110.**

	Adjective	Comparative	Superlative
1 one syllable	small	smaller	the smallest
2 -e	large	larger	the largest
3 -y	easy	easier	the easiest
4 short vowel + consonant	big	bigger	the biggest
5 two or more syllables	popular	more popular	the most popular
6 irregular	good bad far	better worse further	the best the worst the furthest

Sandy's restaurant is **smaller than** The Red Dragon.
Mount Etna is **the smallest** restaurant **in** the town.

3 46.2 **Drill. Listen. Make the comparatives.**

1 It's a noisy restaurant.
 This one's noisier.

2 It's an interesting restaurant.
 This one's more interesting.

4 **Give your opinions. Compare these things. Use the adjectives in brackets.**

I think cats are friendlier than dogs.
OR
I think dogs are friendlier than cats.

1 cats and dogs (friendly)
2 tea and coffee (good)
3 letters and emails (nice)
4 TV and the radio (interesting)
5 English and your language (easy)
6 men and women (tidy)
7 trains and planes (safe)
8 a headache and toothache (bad)
9 football and athletics (popular)
10 the USA and Australia (big)

5 46.3 **Drill. Listen. Give the response.**

1 This is a big restaurant.
 Yes. It's the biggest restaurant in the town.

2 This is an expensive shop.
 Yes. It's the most expensive shop in the town.

6a Your life **What (or Who) is ... ?**

– the largest room in your house
– the most popular sport in your country
– the nicest meal that you've ever had
– the most difficult thing in English
– the most famous person in your country
– the worst school subject
– the best car in the world
– the most expensive thing that you've ever bought
– the best thing that you've ever done
– the worst thing that you've ever done

b **Compare your answers with a partner.**

Now I can ...
compare people, places, and things.

1 Where do you normally shop? Why?
- at the supermarket
- at local shops
- on the Internet
- at the market

2a 47.1 **Listen. Where do the people normally shop? Complete the first column of the table.**

	shops	reasons
1 Peter		
2 Susan		
3 Anjit		
4 Birgit		
5 Troy		

b Listen again. What reasons do the people give? Write the correct letters in the table above. There may be more than one reason.
a It's cheaper.
b The food is fresher.
c I can shop 24/7.
d You can buy everything in one shop.
e It's friendlier and more personal.
f Parking is easier.
g It's more convenient.
h All the small shops have gone.

c Write about each person.

Peter shops ... because ...

> **Language note** *not as ... as*
>
> We use *not as ... as* for comparatives.
>
> 1 The supermarket is cheaper than the local shops.
> The local shops are**n't as cheap as** the supermarket.
> 2 The local shops are friendlier than the supermarket.
> The supermarket is**n't as friendly as** the local shops.

3a What do the people say about these things?
1 Peter – wine
2 Susan – when she was a child
3 Anjit – opening hours
4 Birgit – South Africa
5 Troy – home delivery

b Listen again and check your answers.

4a Your life **Answer these questions.**
1 How often do you shop ... ?
- at a supermarket
- at local shops
- at a street market
- at a shopping centre
- on the Internet
2 Which do you prefer?
3 Where do you normally buy food?
4 Which of the opinions from exercise 2b do you agree with?

b Discuss your answers with a partner.

5a Writing **Read the text about shopping.**

I usually go to the local shops and the market, because I think the food is fresher. **However**, I go to the supermarket for heavy things like sugar and drinks. You can park there easily, **but** it isn't as friendly or personal as the local shops. **On the other hand**, the local shops are often more expensive.

b Write a paragraph about your own shopping habits. Compare the different ways of shopping. Give your reasons.

> ✓ **Now I can ...**
> *compare different kinds of shopping.*

1a `48.1` **Read and listen. What size shirt does the man buy?**

S	M	L	XL
SMALL	MEDIUM	LARGE	EXTRA LARGE

Customer	Excuse me. Can I try this shirt on, please?
Assistant	Yes. The changing rooms are over there.
Customer	Thank you.

Later...

Assistant	How is it?
Customer	It's too tight.
Assistant	What size is that?
Customer	Large. But it isn't big enough. Have you got it in a larger size?
Assistant	Yes. Here you are. This is an extra large.
Customer	Thanks.

Later...

Assistant	Is that any good?
Customer	Yes. This one's fine, thanks. I'll take it.
Assistant	Anything else?
Customer	No, thank you.
Assistant	That's £45 then, please.

b **Practise the conversation with a partner.**

2a **Complete the expressions.**

Everyday expressions **Buying clothes**

Can I t_____ this shirt on, please?
The changing r_____ are over there.
H_____ is it?
W_____ size is that?
Have you got it in a larger s_____?
Is that a_____ good?

b **Check your answers with the conversation in exercise 1.**

Language note *too/enough*

It's **too** tight.   They're **too** loose.

It's **too** small. It isn't big **enough**.

3 **Change the conversation in exercise 1. Start like this.**

Customer: Excuse me. Can I try these shorts on, please?

4a `48.2` **Listen to three conversations. Answer the questions each time.**
1 What does the person try on?
2 What's wrong with it/them?
3 What does he/she ask for?
4 Does he/she get it/them?

b **Work with a partner. Choose one of the conversations.**

5 **Speaking** **Work with a partner. Make new conversations in the clothes shop.**

English in the world
Bargains

What are these signs in your language?

1 Sale 50% off
2 BUY 1 GET 1 FREE
3 Two for the price of one
4 SPECIAL OFFER
5 Buy now Pay later
6 Closing Down Sale Everything Must Go!

Now I can ...
ask about and buy clothes.

1 **49.1** **Listen and repeat.**

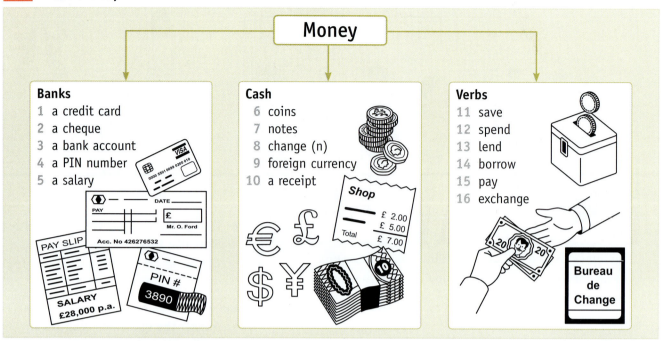

Money

Banks
1 a credit card
2 a cheque
3 a bank account
4 a PIN number
5 a salary

Cash
6 coins
7 notes
8 change (n)
9 foreign currency
10 a receipt

Verbs
11 save
12 spend
13 lend
14 borrow
15 pay
16 exchange

Language note *pay (for / by); lend / borrow*

1 The verb *pay* is used in different ways:
pay a / the bill
pay **for** a meal / some shoes / a ticket
pay **by** credit card / cheque

2 lend (to) = give money and take back
borrow (from) = take money and give back

He **lent** me some money.
I **borrowed** some money from him.
Can you **lend** me £5?
Can I **borrow** £40?

2 **Ask and answer with a partner. Use the cues.**

1 A *Can I pay by credit card, please?*
B *Yes, of course. / No, (I'm) sorry.*

1 pay by credit card
2 borrow some money
3 have the bill
4 exchange some foreign currency
5 have a receipt
6 pay by cheque
7 have some coins for the machine
8 open a bank account
9 pay for these books
10 have my change

3 **49.2** **Listen to eight conversations. What's the problem?**

1 *He hasn't got enough money.*

4 **Your life** **How do people normally do these things in your country? Choose from the different ways in the box.**

in cash   by cheque   by credit card
on the Internet   electronically

1 receive their salary
2 pay bills
3 pay for meals in a restaurant
4 take money abroad
5 send money abroad

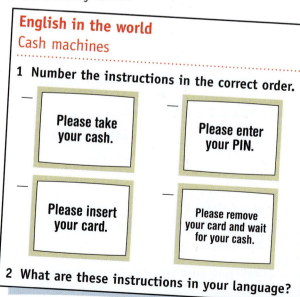

English in the world
Cash machines

1 Number the instructions in the correct order.

Please take your cash.

Please enter your PIN.

Please insert your card.

Please remove your card and wait for your cash.

2 What are these instructions in your language?

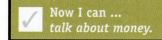

✓ Now I can ...
talk about money.

1 `50.1` **Read and listen.**

Sarah Oh, here's a text from Lucy. She's going to the bank, so she**'ll be** late.

Cindy That's £4.50, please, Peter.

Peter You know, it says in the newspaper that we **won't have** money in the future.

Cindy **Will we pay** for everything with credit cards?

Peter **No, we won't.** People **will pay** for things electronically.

Sarah How **will they do** that?

Peter You**'ll have** a computer chip in your hand. When you want something, you'll just hold out your hand.

Cindy Huh, that won't be new. Our kids do that now!

Can I borrow some money, Mum?

2 **Read the examples. Study the rules on page 111.**

Future with *will*

We use *will* for predictions:
In the future, you**'ll have** a computer chip in your hand.
She**'ll be** late.

People **will pay** electronically. I**'ll be** late.	They **won't use** cash. I **won't arrive** before 7.30.
Will we **use** credit cards?	Yes, we **will**. No, we **won't**.
How **will** we **pay** for things?	When **will** she **arrive**?

3a **Make sentences about the future. Use the cues.**

1 We won't use money.
2 We'll pay for things electronically.

1 use money ✗
2 pay for things electronically ✓
3 buy everything on the Internet ✓
4 go shopping ✗
5 write letters ✗
6 send emails ✓
7 travel to work ✗
8 work from home ✓

b **Work with a partner. Ask and answer.**

1 A *Will we use money?*
  B *No, we won't.*

4a `50.2` **Listen to the messages in Kay's voice mail. Complete the sentences. Use these verbs with *will* or *won't*.**

email	be	need	have
~~arrive~~	miss	phone	fix

1 The visitors *won't arrive* before three o'clock.
2 Farida _____ the photographs.
3 Her husband _____ time to get the theatre tickets.
4 John _____ the meeting.
5 Her mother _____ later.
6 The engineer _____ the computer tomorrow morning.
7 Her son _____ a meal.
8 Margaret _____ here next week.

b **Work with a partner. Ask and answer about the messages.**

1 A *Will the visitors arrive before three o'clock?*
  B *No, they won't.*

5 **Writing Make some predictions about your life in ten years' time. Write six sentences.**

1 I'll be a famous writer.
2 I'll live in a different country …
3 I'll be married/single/divorced …

✓ **Now I can …**
talk about the future.

1a `51.1` **Read and listen. Tick ✓ the topics the people write about.**
- – global warming
- – travel in space
- – computers
- – diseases
- – cars
- – wars

What will the future be like?

1 In the future, I don't think people will have a computer, a mobile phone, a camera and things like that. They'll just have one small computer. It will be as small as a mobile phone and it will be a lot more powerful than today's computers. In fact, it will do everything, like book holidays or order food from the supermarket. You won't need a keyboard. You'll just talk to it. You'll say: 'I want to fly to Moscow on Friday.' Then the computer will buy the tickets. So life will be a lot easier – as long as you don't lose your little computer. *Tadashi, Japan*

2 Will we have cars in the future? Yes, I think we will, but they'll be very different from today's cars. First, they won't use petrol or diesel, because we won't have enough oil in fifty years' time. Cars will probably use electricity or hydrogen. So they'll be quieter and cleaner. And I think the roads will be safer, too, because you won't actually drive your car. You'll just sit in it and the car's computer will drive it. So there won't be any accidents. *Flavia, Brazil*

3 I don't think the world will be a safer place in the future. I think it will be more dangerous – because of diseases. People travel a lot now, so diseases move very quickly from place to place. In the future, travel will be faster and cheaper, because planes will be better. Sooner or later a new and very dangerous disease will appear. It will move quickly from one continent to another and millions of people will die. *Miklos, Hungary*

b Do the writers think life in the future will be better or worse?

2 **What do the writers think will be ... ?**
- – quieter and cleaner
- – smaller and more powerful
- – more dangerous
- – easier
- – safer
- – faster and cheaper

3 **What else do the writers say about these things?**
- – mobile phones
- – computers
- – transport
- – the world's population

> **Language note** **Expressing opinions 2**
> I **think** the world will be safer.
> I **don't think** the world will be safer.
> NOT ~~I think the world won't be safer.~~

4 **Give your opinions. Use the cues.**
1 I think we will drive cars.
   OR I don't think we will drive cars.
1 we / drive / cars
2 the world / be / more dangerous
3 computers / do / everything for us
4 millions of people / die / from diseases
5 cars / use / electricity
6 global warming / destroy / the earth
7 we / have / wars
8 people / take / holidays in space

5 **Speaking** **Write six questions about the future. Interview a partner. Find reasons for his/her opinions.**
A *Will the world be safer in the future?*
B *No, I think it will be more dangerous.*
A *Why?*

> **Pronunciation**
> Sentence stress
> ....
> 1 `51.2` **Listen.**
>   I'll be <u>late</u>   I'll be <u>late</u> for the <u>meeting</u>.
>
> 2 `51.3` **Listen and repeat.**
>   I'll see you   I'll see you this evening.
>   We'll be there   We'll be there at ten.

> ✓ **Now I can ...**
> *make predictions about the future.*

1 Look back at Episodes 5 and 6. What happened?

2 `52.1` Read and listen to the story. What do Ryan and Cindy decide to do? Why?

3 Complete the sentences.

1 _Melanie_ wants to stay at university.
2 _____ are still empty.
3 _____ wants to open a new café.
4 _____ is losing money.
5 _____ is still looking for a shop.
6 _____ won't give Ryan and Cindy a loan.
7 _____ thinks Anna's offer is OK.
8 _____ wants to live in Spain.
9 _____ doesn't want to leave her friends.
10 _____ don't have any money.

4a Complete the expressions.

> **Everyday expressions**
> **Talking about money problems**
>
> How much w_____ that cost?
> We c_____ afford it.
> Business isn't v_____ good.
> It's losing m_____.
> It isn't a b_____ price.
> We're b_____.

b Use the expressions. Complete these conversations.

1 **A** We need a new car.
 B How _____?
 A About £15,000.
 B _____.
 A Why not?
 B We're _____.

2 **A** They've had an offer for the café.
 B Yes, and it _____.
 A But why do they want to sell it?
 B _____.
 A Really? Why is it losing money?
 B _____.

5 Language check. <u>Underline</u> the examples of the future with _will_ in the story.

6 Work in a group. Practise the story.

1

Cindy There's an email here from Melanie. She wants to do another year at university.
Russell How much will that cost?
Cindy A lot. And we can't afford it. Business isn't very good.
Russell Why's that?
Cindy The factory has closed and Peter's old offices are still empty, so we've lost a lot of customers.
Russell A big company wants to open an Internet café in those offices.
Cindy I know, and that will be the end for us.
Russell What does Dad think?
Cindy He wants to sell The Coffee Shop, but who'll buy it when it's losing money?
Russell Anna's looking for a place for her shop. Maybe she'll buy it.

2 _Three weeks later..._

Cindy Will the bank give us a loan?
Ryan No, they won't, but we've had an offer from Anna Harlow. Look.
Cindy Well, it isn't a bad price, but where will we live, Ryan? The café's our home, too.
Ryan We'll open a bar on the Costa del Sol in Spain! I've always wanted to do that.
Cindy But all our friends are here, Ryan.
Ryan What else can we do? We're broke!

3 OK. We'll sell The Coffee Shop to Anna.

> ✓ Now I can ...
> _talk about money problems._

1 `53.1` **Listen and repeat.**

1 clubbing

2 mountain-climbing

3 sailing

4 scuba-diving

5 water-skiing

6 canoeing

7 going to the gym

8 sunbathing

9 going out with friends

10 relaxing

11 collecting things

12 doing DIY

13 painting

14 sightseeing

15 surfing the Internet

Language note *-ing*

When we talk about activities, we use the *-ing* form with no article.
I've never tried water-ski**ing**.
NOT ~~I've never tried water-ski.~~
Scuba-div**ing** is great.
NOT ~~The scuba-diving is great.~~

2 `53.2` **Drill. Listen. Ask the question.**

1 sunbathe
   Do you like sunbathing?

3 **Ask and answer with a partner about the activities. Follow the pattern.**

A Do you like ...-ing?
B Yes, I do. I love it. / I think it's great.
   I've never tried it, but it looks
      exciting / interesting / dangerous.
   I don't know, but I'd like to try it.
   I don't mind it.
   No, I don't. I can't stand it. / I think
      it's boring.

4 **What other leisure activities do you know? Put them in a table like this.**

playing	doing	(other verbs + *-ing*)
tennis	karate	gardening

5 `53.3` **Listen. What do the people like? Complete the table.**

	Arnold	Beth
likes		
doesn't mind		
doesn't like		
hasn't tried		

6 **Your life** **Complete the sentences about your own life.**

1 I love _____.
2 I don't like _____.
3 I don't mind _____.
4 I've never tried _____.
5 I'd like to try _____.

Now I can ...
talk about activities.

1 54.1 Read and listen.

The best times of year in Japan are spring and autumn.

If you **come** in April, you**'ll see** the cherry blossom. It's really beautiful.

Most visitors go to the Mediterranean in July and August, so the beaches are often very crowded.

However, the beaches **won't be** crowded if you **go** in June or September.

2 Read the examples. Study the rules on page 112.

First conditional

We use a first conditional to talk about real conditions in the future.

    an *if* clause   **a main clause**
If **you come** in April, **you'll see** the cherry blossom.
    a main clause   **an *if* clause**
You'll see the cherry blossom if **you come** in April.

NOT ~~You'll see the cherry blossom if you will come in April.~~

3 Put the verbs in brackets into the correct tense.

1 If we _book_ on the Internet, it _will be_ cheaper. (book/be)
2 You ____ a cheaper holiday if you ____ it now. (get/book)
3 If we ____ on Wednesday, the airport ____ busy. (travel/not be)
4 You ____ the best weather if you ____ in June. (have/come)
5 You ____ a visa if you ____ an EU passport. (not need/have)
6 If you ____ by train, it ____ longer. (travel/take)
7 If you ____ in winter, it ____ too hot. (go/not be)
8 You ____ vaccinations if you ____ to go to Africa. (need/want)

Language note *when*

I'll phone you **if** the plane is late.
(future possibility)
I'll phone you **when** I get there.
(future certainty)

4a 54.2 Listen. Match the cues.

1 collect the tickets _c_
2 phone you ____
3 look for a hotel ____
4 send you a postcard ____
5 book the holiday ____
6 take a taxi ____

a arrive
b go to the airport
c have my lunch break
d leave the office
e go on holiday
f go into town

b Write the sentences.

1 *I'll collect the tickets when I have my lunch break.*

5a Speaking Complete these sentences with your own ideas.

1 If I'm ill tomorrow, _I won't go to work_.
2 If the weather is nice on Sunday, ____.
3 If I stay in this evening, ____.
4 When I get home tonight, ____.
5 When I leave work tomorrow, ____.
6 If it rains on Saturday, ____.
7 When I go on holiday this year, ____.
8 If I haven't got enough money at the end of the week, ____.

b Compare your answers with a partner. Are any of your answers the same?

Pronunciation
won't and *want*

1 54.3 Listen and repeat.
  1 We won't be there.
    We want to be there.
  2 We won't go by train.
    We want to go by train.

2 54.4 Listen. Do you hear *want* or *won't* each time?

 Now I can ... *talk about future possibilities and certainties.*

1 **55.1** **Read and listen. Match the texts with the correct pictures.**

a   b   c   d

If you want to try a different holiday this year, you'll find some great ideas in our holiday guide.

DREAM HOLIDAYS

1 With its blue sea and beautiful islands, Croatia is the place for a sailing holiday. On a one-week course you'll learn how to sail a yacht while you travel along the coast from island to island. You'll live on the yacht with your teacher and the other students, and you'll sail about thirty kilometres a day. You'll stop at a different town for dinner and some sightseeing each night.

2 Do you want to change your life? Then a holiday at the Chiva-Som resort in Thailand will help. You'll stay at the famous Chiva-Som Hotel by the sea. Here you can relax and forget all your problems. You can try yoga and tai chi or have a massage. The food is delicious and very healthy. You can also do a course in Thai cooking.

3 If you like dancing, then you'll love a trip to Cuba with Club Dance Holidays. In the mornings you'll learn how to dance the tango and other dances. At night you'll go dancing at Havana's famous clubs. You'll stay at the five-star Hotel Nacionál. If you stay for an extra week, you'll have the chance to explore Cuba's wonderful rainforests and beaches.

4 Scuba-diving will take you to a new world. You'll stay at the Rosetta Hotel in Sharm el-Sheikh, Egypt. Before you go into the sea, you'll learn how to scuba-dive in the hotel's swimming pool. Then you'll move into the warm water of the Red Sea with its beautiful coral reefs and tropical fish. When you aren't in the water, there will be flights to some of Egypt's ancient monuments.

2 **Find this information about each holiday.**
1 Where is the holiday?
2 Where do you stay?
3 What is the main activity?
4 What other things can you do?

Language note **Time clauses**

We can use the first conditional structure with time clauses that start with *when, before, after, while*:
1 I'll phone you **when** I get to the airport.
2 **Before** we go to the travel agent's, we'll check the Internet.
3 I'm sure these postcards will arrive **after** we get home.
4 I'll look after the bags **while** you go swimming.

---

3 **What do these adjectives describe in the texts?**

1 blue	5 wonderful
2 beautiful	6 warm
3 famous	7 tropical
4 delicious	8 ancient

4a **Your life** **Answer the questions.**
1 Where do you normally go on holiday?
2 When do you go?
3 How long do you stay for?
4 Who do you go with?
5 Where do you stay?
6 What things do you do?

b **Use the questions. Ask and answer with a partner.**

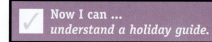
✓ **Now I can ...**
understand a holiday guide.

1a 56.1 **Read and listen.**

Receptionist	Good morning, The Dorset Hotel.
Caller	Hello. I'd like to make a reservation, please.
Receptionist	Certainly. When for?
Caller	For 18 July.
Receptionist	How many nights?
Caller	Three nights.
Receptionist	Just one moment. Yes, that's fine. How many guests will there be?
Caller	Two – me and my husband.
Receptionist	And would you like a double or a twin room?
Caller	A double, please. And we'd like a room with a sea view, please.
Receptionist	Yes, that will be fine. The price will be £85 per night.
Caller	Does that include breakfast?
Receptionist	Yes, it does. So what name is it, please?
Caller	It's Mr and Mrs Taylor. Will you confirm the reservation by email?
Receptionist	Yes, of course.

b **Practise the conversation with a partner.**

2a **Complete the expressions.**

Everyday expressions **Booking a hotel room**
I'd like to _____ a reservation, please.
When _____?
How _____ nights?
_____ many guests will there be?
We'd _____ a room with a sea view.
Does that _____ breakfast?
What _____ is it, please?

b **Who says each thing – the caller or the receptionist?**

3a 56.2 **Listen to two more conversations. Complete the table.**

	The Angel	Hotel Jumbo
Name		
Arrival		
No. of nights		
No. of guests		
Type of room		
Price per night		
Breakfast included		

b **Work with a partner. Make the conversations. Use the information in the table.**

4a **Writing** **Read the email.**

To: taylor425@world.com

Subject: Confirmation of reservation

Dear Mrs Taylor

This is to confirm your reservation at our hotel for 18 July for three nights. The reservation is for two people in a double room with a sea view.

The price will be £85 per night including breakfast.

We look forward to welcoming you to our hotel.

Yours sincerely,

M Barker
Manager

b **Write an email to confirm one of the reservations in exercise 3.**

English in the world
Hotel signs

What are these signs in your language?

1 RECEPTION
2 VACANCIES
3 DO NOT DISTURB
4 Please leave keys at reception
5 Lobby
6 Bed & Breakfast

Now I can ...
make and confirm hotel reservations.

1a `57.1` **Listen and repeat.**

1 a filing cabinet
2 a photocopier
6 a shelf
5 a printer
3 a waste bin
4 a cupboard

b What other things in the picture can you name?

2 Complete the expressions with the correct verbs.

do   send   use   go   have   make

Office activities

1	an email
2	a letter
3	an appointment
4	a phone call
5	some filing
6	some photocopying
7	to a meeting
8	on the Internet
9	a break
10	a day off
11	the computer
12	the fax machine

3a Write the past simple of the verbs in exercise 2.

send – sent

b `57.2` **Drill. Listen. Say what you did.**

1 an appointment
   I made an appointment.

4a `57.3` **Listen. Why isn't Sayeed wearing a suit?**

Sayeed   Josh

b Listen again. Number the things that Josh did in the correct order.

___ went to a meeting
___ sent some emails
___ made a couple of appointments
___ had a break
___ went on the Internet
_1_ made a few phone calls
___ did some filing

5a `Your life` **Did you do any of the things in exercise 2 yesterday? What other things did you do?**

b Speaking Work with a partner. Talk about your day yesterday. Try to get more information.

A *How was your day yesterday?*
B *It was great / OK / fine / terrible / not very good.*
A *What did you do?*
B *...*
A *Really? / Oh, right. / Why did you do that? / Was it good?*

Now I can ...
talk about everyday office activities.

1 `58.1` **Read and listen.**

Daniel Well, I **must** go. I **have to** make some phone calls.

Lucy Me, too. I have to photocopy this report.

Daniel Oh, there's something wrong with the photocopier. We **mustn't** use it.

Lucy But Olive **has to** have the report for a meeting today.

Daniel Well, take it to The Photo Shop.

Lucy Good idea, but I must hurry. The meeting's at 12 and I mustn't be late.

Later...

Lucy. The meeting's going to be next week now, so you **don't have to** photocopy that report today.

2 **Read the examples. Study the rules on page 112.**

have to/must/mustn't		
I **have to** send an email. I **must** hurry.	=	Do it. It's necessary.
You **mustn't** use the phone.	=	Don't use it. It isn't allowed.

3 **Say what you *must* or *mustn't* do.**

1 You mustn't use the lift. You must take the stairs.

1 Don't use the lift. Take the stairs.

2 Park between the white lines. Don't park on the yellow lines.

3 Stop when the light is red. Don't stop on the crossing.

4 Put all paper in the bin. Don't put bottles or food in the bin.

5 Don't use the office phone for personal calls. Use your mobile.

4 **Read the examples. Study the rules on page 112.**

mustn't/don't have to
You **mustn't** go. = Don't go. It isn't allowed.
You **don't have to** go. = It isn't necessary. You can go if you want to.

5 **Complete the sentences with *mustn't* or *don't have to*.**

1 You _mustn't_ turn left here.

2 You _____ turn right here.

3 You _____ pay by credit card.

4 You _____ smoke here.

5 You _____ pay.

6 You _____ drink the water.

6a **Writing** Write six sentences about your life with *have to/don't have to*.

1 I have to/don't have to get up early on Saturdays.

b Write six rules for your home.

1 You mustn't smoke.

2 You must ...

Pronunciation
must / mustn't

`58.2` **We don't usually pronounce the *t* in *must*. Listen and repeat.**

1 I must go.

2 You mustn't do that.

3 We must leave.

4 We mustn't swim here.

5 I must get up.

6 You mustn't smoke.

7 You must be careful.

8 We mustn't go out.

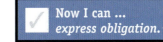

Now I can ...
express obligation.

1 `59.1` **Listen. Choose the correct city for each speaker.**

__ Kuala Lumpur

__ New York

__ Venice

2 Listen again. Complete the table.

	1	2	3
How does he/she travel to work?			
How long does it take?			
What problems does he/she mention?			

Language note **Time expressions**

How long does the journey take?
It takes ... – an hour
– half an hour
– an hour and a half
– an hour and a quarter
– a couple of hours
– two and a half hours.

3a Complete the text for speaker 1.

1 He lives near _____. He works in _____. He walks
to the station and he takes the train to _____.
Then he _____. The journey takes about _____. The
journey is OK, but in the summer _____.

b Write texts for speakers 2 and 3.

4a `Your life` **Answer these questions.**

1 Where do you live?
2 Where do you work/study?
3 How do you travel to work/school/university? Why?
4 How long does the journey take?
5 What things do you do on the journey?
6 What problems do you sometimes have?

b Ask and answer with a partner. Compare your journeys.

English in the world
Rush hour

In Britain, the busiest times for transport are:
7.30–9.15 a.m. The morning **rush hour**. People go to
work, and children go to school. There are often long
traffic jams.
2.45–4 p.m. Children come home from school. A lot of
parents take their children to and from school by car.
We call this **the school run**.
5–6.30 p.m. The evening rush hour. People go home
from work. The trains and buses are usually very
crowded and a lot of people have to stand.

Compare this with your country.

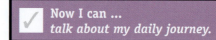

✓ **Now I can ...**
talk about my daily journey.

60

ENGLISH FOR EVERYDAY LIFE
That's Life! Episode 8

1 Look back at Episodes 6 and 7. What happened?

2 **60.1** Read and listen to the story. What do Sarah and Jordan find?

3 Answer the questions.
   1 Where are Jordan and Sarah?
   2 Where is Sarah going?
   3 What has Sarah brought for Jordan?
   4 What is Jordan doing?
   5 Who do the laptops belong to?
   6 Who is Anna Harlow?
   7 What is the email about?
   8 Why doesn't Jordan want to open the email?
   9 Why does he open it?
   10 What does Sarah do when she reads it?

4a Complete the expressions.

> **Everyday expressions**
> **Greeting a visitor**
>
> Come _____ in.
> This is _____ surprise.
> It's nice _____ see you.
> Take _____ seat.
> Let _____ get you (a cup of coffee).

 b Work with a partner. Make conversations.
   A You have come to see B.
   B Welcome A.
   A Say why you have come.
   B Invite A to sit down and offer a drink.
   A Accept or refuse the drink.
   B Respond.

5 Language check. <u>Underline</u> examples of *must / mustn't* or *(don't) have to* in the story.

6 Work in a group. Practise the story.

Sarah Hello!
Jordan Oh, hi, Sarah. Come on in. This is a surprise.
Sarah I'm going to the university, but I don't have to be there till 3.30.
Jordan Well, it's nice to see you. Take a seat. Let me get you a cup of coffee.
Sarah You don't have to do that. I've brought some coffee and some doughnuts.
Jordan Sarah, you're wonderful. Peter's a lucky man.

Sarah You look busy.
Jordan Yes. We have to check these laptops from Starlight Properties.
Sarah They bought Peter's old offices.
Jordan Yes. There's a problem with the email program on this one. It ...
Sarah Look! There's an email from Anna Harlow. That's Russell's girlfriend.
Jordan Oh, yes. Subject: 'The Coffee Shop'. Why is she writing to Starlight about that?
Sarah Well, come on. Let's have a look at it.
Jordan No, we mustn't open emails.
Sarah I won't give you your coffee and doughnut if you don't open it.
Jordan You're a hard woman, Sarah. I hope Peter knows!

Oh, no! I don't believe it.

Peter. I'm at Jordan's workshop. You must come here quickly!

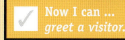

Now I can ...
greet a visitor.

1 61.1 Listen and repeat.

1 a washing machine

2 a dishwasher

3 a microwave

4 a toaster

5 a kettle

6 a vacuum cleaner

7 a hairdryer

8 a shaver

9 a clock radio

10 a DVD player

11 a light bulb

12 a heater

13 an electric fan

14 an air conditioner

2 61.2 Drill. Listen. Where are the things?

1 We're looking for a DVD player.
The DVD players are over there.

3 Where do you use the things in exercise 1? Write them in the table.

living room	*DVD player*
kitchen	*microwave*
bathroom	
bedroom	

4 Complete the expressions with the verbs.

cook do lay tidy
take out clean make

1 _____ the beds
   breakfast
2 _____ the shopping
   the washing-up
   the ironing
3 _____ the room
   the garden
4 _____ the windows
   the car
5 _____ the dinner
6 _____ the table
7 _____ the rubbish

Language note
Subject /object questions

Do you do the washing-up?
What jobs **do you do** in the house?
BUT
Who **does** the ironing?
Who **makes** the beds?

5a Your life Look at the household jobs in exercise 4. Which ones do you do?

b Ask and answer with a partner.

Do you make the beds?
OR *Who makes the beds in your house?*

Now I can ...
talk about things and jobs in the home.

1 `62.1` **Read and listen.**

SAFETY IN THE HOME

1 You **shouldn't** stand on a chair to reach things.

You **should** use a stepladder.

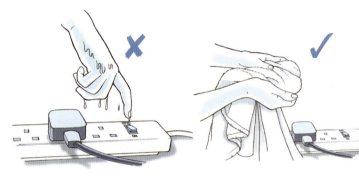

2 You **shouldn't** touch electrical things with wet hands.

You **should** dry your hands first.

2 Read the examples. Study the rules on page 112.

should / shouldn't		
We use *should* and *shouldn't* + verb for advice.		
You **should** use a stepladder.	=	Use a stepladder. It's safer.
You **shouldn't** stand on a chair.	=	Don't stand on a chair. It's dangerous.
NOT ~~You shouldn't to use a stepladder.~~		

3 Complete the sentences with *You should* or *You shouldn't*.

1 _____ put a lot of salt on your food.
2 _____ eat fruit and vegetables.
3 _____ do some exercise every day.
4 _____ smoke.
5 _____ drive when you're tired.
6 _____ laugh a lot.
7 _____ drink alcohol and drive.
8 _____ sleep for seven or eight hours a night.

4a Match the advice with the problems.

1 I'm very tired. *e*
2 I've got toothache. __
3 I feel ill. __
4 It's cold in here. __
5 I'm broke. __
6 It's raining. __
7 I've lost my wallet. __
8 The police stopped me today. __

a Don't leave the window open.
b Take an umbrella.
c Don't go to work today.
d Phone the police.
e Go to bed.
f Don't drive so fast.
g Go to the dentist's.
h Look for a job.

b Work with a partner. Ask and answer. Use *You should* or *You shouldn't*.

A *What's wrong?*
B *I'm very tired.*
A *You should go to bed.*

5a `Your life` Write two pieces of advice for these things. Use *should / shouldn't*.

– a healthy life
– safety in the home
– saving money
– safety on the roads

b Compare your ideas with a partner.

English in the world
Warning signs

What are these signs in your language?

1 DANGER! Do not touch
2 TAKE CARE! Very hot water
3 Mind your head
4 CAUTION! Floor may be slippery

Now I can ... understand and give advice.

1 **63.1** **Read and listen to the text. Answer the questions.**

1 Which country is it about?
2 What does the new law say?

I promise to love,
honour, and wash up

Who does the housework? Who looks after children and old people?

 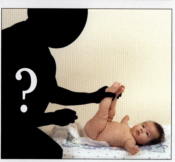

In most couples it's probably 'the wife', but one country wants to change that. That country is Spain. At the moment, 40 per cent of Spanish men say that they don't do any housework. Their wives, however, spend six hours a day on it. In 2005 the Spanish Parliament passed a new law. Now husbands have to share jobs in the home.

In a café in Madrid we asked people about the law. Conchita Rodriguez: 'Most women go out to work. So, in my opinion, they shouldn't do all the housework too, but they usually do. That isn't fair.'

Juan Salgado: 'Yes, it's a good idea, but I think a lot of men already help in the house. I cook and I take the children to school, so it won't change anything for me and my wife.'

Laura Pino: 'I go out to work, but I prefer to do the housework. I don't want my husband in the kitchen. He repairs the car and takes out the rubbish. I cook and clean. It's simple.'

Pablo Calvache is getting married soon: 'It's OK for women,' he says. 'They learn how to cook and iron when they're young, but we don't. I don't know how to do those things.'

Margarita Uria is a member of the Spanish Parliament. She produced the new law. She agrees. 'Men don't help in the house,' she says. 'But it isn't all their fault. We women should teach them when they're children.'

Will it work? Laura Pino doesn't think so: 'If the man doesn't help, what will his wife do – take him to the police station?'

But Conchita Rodriguez is more positive. 'It will probably happen slowly, but as more women go out to work, things must change.'

2 **Are these statements true (T) or false (F)?**

1 Forty per cent of Spanish men help with the housework.
2 Married women in Spain spend six hours a day on housework.
3 The Spanish Parliament made the new law in 2005.
4 The people are in a café in Madrid.
5 They're all women.
6 All the people in the café think the law is a good idea.

3 **Match two facts with each name.**

Conchita Rodriguez _d_ __
Juan Salgado __ __
Laura Pino __ __
Pablo Calvache __ __
Margarita Uria __ __

a can't cook.
b doesn't want her husband's help with the cooking.
c introduced the new law.
d says it isn't right at the moment.
e thinks boys should learn how to cook.
f thinks the law won't change his life.
g doesn't think the law will work.
h will soon have a wife.
i says that he already does housework.
j doesn't think things will change quickly.

Language note **Expressing opinions 3**
In my opinion, ...   It's a good idea. I (don't) think that...   I (don't) agree.   I (don't) think so.

4 **Your life** **Think about the opinions in the text. Discuss with the class.**

1 Which opinions do you agree with?
2 Is the Spanish law a good idea?
3 Do men and women share domestic jobs in your country?

5 **Writing** **Use the text. Write a paragraph expressing your opinions.**

In my country, men and women _____.
I (don't) think the Spanish law is a good idea, because _____. I (don't) agree with _____. I think _____. I (don't) think the law will work, because _____.

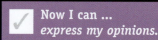
Now I can ...
express my opinions.

1 `64.1` **Listen and repeat.**

1 It isn't working.

2 It's damaged.

3 It's scratched.

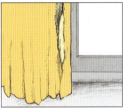

4 It's torn.

5 It's leaking.

6 It's got a hole in it.

2a `64.2` **Read and listen.**

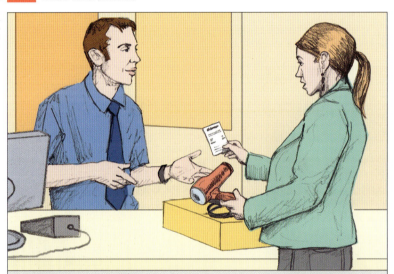

Assistant Hello. Can I help you?

Customer Yes, I bought this hairdryer yesterday, but it isn't working.

Assistant Oh, I'm sorry about that. Would you like to exchange it?

Customer Yes, please.

Assistant Just a moment. ... I'm sorry, we haven't got any more like that.

Customer Oh well, can I have a refund, then, please?

Assistant Yes, of course. Have you got the receipt?

Customer Yes. Here you are.

Assistant Thank you.

b Practise the conversation with a partner.

3 Complete the expressions.

> **Everyday expressions**
> **Dealing with faults**
>
> I b_____ this hairdryer yesterday.
> It isn't w_____ .
> I'm s_____ about that.
> Would you like to e_____ it?
> Can I have a r_____, please?
> Have you got the r_____?

4a `64.3` **Listen to four conversations. Answer the questions each time.**

1 What did he/she buy?
2 When did he/she buy it?
3 What's wrong with it?
4 Does he/she exchange it or get a refund?

b Work with a partner. Make the conversations. Use the information in exercise 4a.

Assistant Hello. Can I help you?

Customer Yes, I bought this jumper at the weekend, but it's got a hole in it.

5 Speaking Work with a partner. Make new conversations for these situations.

1 You bought a camera. It isn't working.
2 You bought a saucepan. It's leaking.
3 You bought a toaster. It's scratched.
4 You bought a DVD player. It's damaged.
5 You bought a sheet. It's torn.

> **Pronunciation**
> Negative auxiliary verbs
>
> **1** `64.4` **Listen.**
>
> | one syllable | two syllables |
> | --- | --- |
> | won't | shouldn't |
>
> **2 Put the words in the correct column.**
> doesn't don't can't mustn't isn't
> aren't wasn't weren't haven't hasn't
>
> **3** `64.5` **Listen, check, and repeat.**

> ✓ **Now I can ...**
> *describe faults with everyday items.*

1 **65.1** Listen and repeat.

1 wood

2 paper

3 metal

4 gold

5 silver

6 cardboard

7 plastic

8 cotton

9 wool

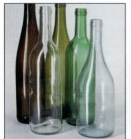
10 glass

11 leather

12 rubber

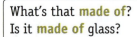
What's that **made of**?
Is it **made of** glass?

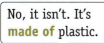
No, it isn't. It's **made of** plastic.

2 Think of something that is made of each material.

Pencils are made of wood.

> **Language note** **Word building 4**
>
> This belt is made of leather.
> It's **a leather belt**.
> BUT
> a **wooden** toy (wood)
> **woollen** gloves (wool)

3 **65.2** Drill. Listen. Say the sentence.
1 These cups are made of paper.
   They're paper cups.
2 This door is made of glass.
   It's a glass door.

4 Describe some of the things around you.
– things that you're wearing
   a silver watch
– things in your classroom
   a wooden desk
– things in your bag, briefcase, or pockets
   a leather purse

5 **65.3** Listen. Which of the materials in exercise 1 does the man mention?

6 **Your life** Discuss these questions.
1 What things do you recycle?
2 Where do you take them?
3 Why should people recycle things?

> **Pronunciation**
> Sentence stress
> ....
> **65.4** Listen and repeat.
> 1 It's made of leather.
> 2 It's made of glass.
> 3 They're made of cotton.
> 4 It's made of gold.
> 5 They're made of metal.

> ✓ **Now I can ...**
> *say what things are made of.*

66 GRAMMAR
Passives

1 `66.1` **Read and listen.**

Nick Kool makes models. He doesn't make them for a hobby. The models **are made** by Nick and his colleagues for TV programmes. Each model **is built** very carefully, but most of them **are destroyed**.

This street **was seen** in a history programme. Several models **were needed** for the programme. It took over four weeks to make each model, but they were destroyed in seconds.

'Everything **is checked** again and again,' says Nick. 'You don't get a second chance.'

2 **Read the examples. Study the rules on page 113.**

Passives	
Active	Nick makes the models.
Passive	The models **are made** by Nick.
Active	Nick checks a model again and again.
Passive	A model **is checked** again and again by Nick.
Each pair of sentences has the same meaning.	

3 **Make sentences about Nick's work. Use the cues.**

1 Photographs are studied.

1 Photographs / study
2 The models / plan
3 The buildings / make
4 They / paint
5 An explosion / produce
6 The model / destroy
7 The explosion / film
8 The programme / see on TV

4a **Read the examples. Study the rules on page 113.**

Past simple passive
We can use the passive in any tense.
Present
The model **is checked** very carefully.
The models **are used** in TV programmes.
Past
The model **was checked** very carefully.
The models **were used** in a TV programme last year.

b **Change the sentences in exercise 3 into the past tense.**

1 Photographs were studied.

5a **Nick is talking about one of the models. Put the verbs into the past simple passive.**

The model in this picture [1]*was built* (build) one sixth of normal size. I can't show you the model, because it [2]_____ (destroy) for a TV programme. It [3]_____ (make) from wood and paper. The buildings and streets [4]_____ (build) first. Then the small things [5]_____ (add). Children's toys [6]_____ (use) for things like bicycles and plants. Shop signs [7]_____ (paint) by hand. These small things are very important. When the model [8]_____ (see) on TV, people thought it was real. The street [9]_____ (use) in a history programme. It [10]_____ (show) on TV last year.

b `66.2` **Listen and check.**

6a **Speaking** **Answer the questions.**

1 What things are produced in your country?
2 Are the things sold to other countries?
3 Where were your clothes made?
4 Where was your car / TV made?
5 Where were your shoes made?
6 Where was your watch made?

b **Ask two people in your class. Compare their answers with yours.**

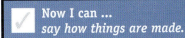

Now I can ...
say how things are made.

1 `67.1` **Listen. Which country is each festival celebrated in?**

1 Loy Krathong

2 The Day of the Dead

3 Maslenitsa

2 Listen again. Write the number of the festival with the correct answers. Some answers are not needed.

1 Why is each festival celebrated?
- _____ to say thank you for the sun
- _____ to remember dead friends and relatives
- _____ to say goodbye to winter
- _____ to celebrate the new year
- _____ to say thank you for water

2 When is each festival celebrated?
- _____ at the end of the rainy season
- _____ on the second Sunday in November
- _____ at the beginning of winter
- _____ on 2 November
- _____ at the end of winter

3a Answer these questions about each festival.

1 What do the people make?
2 What are the things made from?
3 What happens to the things?
4 Are any special kinds of food eaten?

b Listen again and check.

4 **Writing** Write about a festival in your country. Follow the pattern.

I'm from _____ (*country*). My favourite festival is _____ (*name*). It's celebrated _____ (*when?*). It's to _____ (*why?*). For the festival, _____ are made from _____. They are _____ (*What do people do with the things?*). People eat lots of _____ and they _____ (*What things do they do?*). I like _____, because _____ (*How do you feel about the festival?*).

English in the world
Greetings cards
....

The average person in Britain sends 53 greetings cards every year. Most of them (85%) are bought by women. Cards are usually sent for:
- birthdays
- Christmas
- Valentine's Day
- Mother's Day
- Father's Day
- anniversaries
- weddings
- births
- deaths
- passing exams.

Compare this with your country.

67

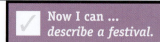

Now I can ...
describe a festival.

1 Look back at Episodes 7 and 8. What happened?

2 68.1 Read and listen to the story. Who must Peter, Sarah, and Jordan stop?

3 Answer the questions.

1 Who bought Peter's old offices?
2 When was the factory sold?
3 What other things did Starlight buy?
4 What does Starlight want to do?
5 Why do they need The Coffee Shop?
6 Are Starlight going to open a new café?
7 Who are Cindy and Ryan going to sell The Coffee Shop to?
8 Who owns Starlight Properties?
9 Why does Anna Harlow want The Coffee Shop?
10 Where are Cindy and Ryan going?

4a Complete the expressions.

> **Everyday expressions**
> **Responding to information**
>
> Yes, that's r_____.
> Oh, I didn't k_____ that.
> Are you s_____?
> Yes, y_____ right.
> That's t_____.

b Use the expressions. Complete the conversation.

A We've got an exam today.
B A_____?
A Yes, the teacher told us on Friday.
B Oh, _____. I wasn't here.
A Look, it's here in my notebook.
B Y_____. Is it on the passive?
A Y_____.
B Oh dear. And the passive isn't easy.
A T_____.

5 Language check. <u>Underline</u> examples of the passive in the story.

6 Work in a group. Practise the story.

Jordan Look at this map, Peter. Your old offices here were sold to Starlight Properties.
Peter Yes, that's right.
Sarah This factory and all the other properties in the block were sold last year, too.
Jordan And they were all bought by Starlight.
Peter Oh, I didn't know that.
Jordan Well, it was done very quietly.
Sarah Starlight wants to build a big shopping centre, it seems.
Peter Are you sure?
Jordan Yes, it's all here in the computer.
Peter I see. And now Starlight owns the whole block.
Sarah Except The Coffee Shop. And without The Coffee Shop, they can't build their shopping centre.

Peter But aren't Starlight going to open a new café?
Jordan No. They just said that so that Cindy and Ryan will sell The Coffee Shop.
Sarah And it's worked.
Peter Yes, you're right. But they aren't selling it to Starlight. They're selling it to Anna Harlow.
Jordan That's true, but Starlight Properties is owned by Anna Harlow's family.
Sarah She doesn't want to open a shop. She's just buying the property for Starlight.
Peter Well, we must stop her!

 Meanwhile...

Bye, Russell. We're going to sign the contract to sell the café.

✓ **Now I can ...**
respond to what people say.

1 69.1 **Listen and repeat.**

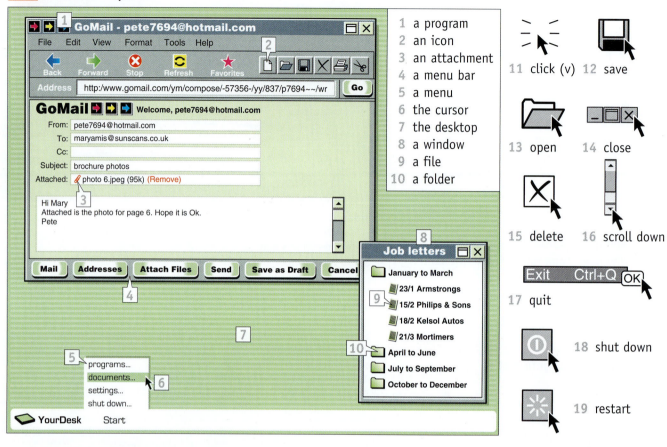

1 a program
2 an icon
3 an attachment
4 a menu bar
5 a menu
6 the cursor
7 the desktop
8 a window
9 a file
10 a folder

11 click (v)   12 save
13 open   14 close
15 delete   16 scroll down
17 quit
18 shut down
19 restart

2 **Complete the instructions with these verbs.**

1 *Save / Restart* your work.
2 *Scroll down / Quit* the program.
3 *Click on / Save* the icon.
4 *Delete / Shut down* the file.
5 *Save / Scroll down* the menu.
6 *Shut down / Close* the computer.
7 *Restart / Open* the computer.

3 69.2 **Drill. Listen. Say the sentence.**

1 Click on the icon.
   OK. I've clicked on the icon.

2 Quit that program.
   OK. I've quit that program.

4 69.3 **Listen. Someone is phoning a computer helpline. Number the words in the order that you hear them.**

__ file   _1_ desktop
__ menu bar   __ window
__ icon   __ save
__ restart   __ program
__ quit   __ scroll down

5 Your life **Work with a partner. Discuss these questions.**

1 What do you use computers for?
2 Do you like using computers?
3 How did you learn how to use a computer?
4 What kind of computer do you use?

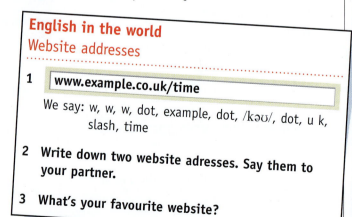

English in the world
Website addresses

1 www.example.co.uk/time

We say: w, w, w, dot, example, dot, /kəʊ/, dot, u k, slash, time

2 **Write down two website adresses. Say them to your partner.**

3 **What's your favourite website?**

Now I can ...
talk about computers.

1 **70.1** **Read and listen.**

Jordan I've fixed the computer **which wasn't working**.

Cindy Thanks, Jordan. Ryan! Where are the things **that you bought from the supermarket**?

Ryan They're in the car. I'll get them in a minute.

Cindy Oh, he's so slow.

Jordan You should read the article **that's in the paper today**. It's about people **who do things slowly**.

Cindy Really?

Jordan Yes, it says people **who do things quickly** make a lot of mistakes. People **that are slow** enjoy life – and are more successful.

Cindy Well, if that's true, I'm married to the most successful man in the world!

2 **Read the examples. Study the rules on page 113.**

> **Relative clauses**
>
> **1 Relative clauses give us more information about people and things.**
> I've fixed the computer.
> I've fixed the computer **which wasn't working**.
> It's about people.
> It's about people **who do things slowly**.
>
> **2 A relative clause usually starts with a relative pronoun.**
> People **who**/**that are slow** enjoy life.
> You should read the article **which**/**that is in the paper**.

3 **Complete the sentences. Use *who* or *which*.**

1 Where's the letter _which_ arrived today?
2 That's one of the students _____ studies with Sarah.
3 Have you got the magazine _____ was on the table?
4 People _____ do things quickly don't enjoy life.
5 He's the man _____ fixes our computers.
6 Where's the photocopier _____ isn't working?
7 That's the film _____ was on TV last week.
8 Are they the people _____ go jogging with you?

4 **Read the examples. Study the rules on page 113.**

> **Relative clauses: subject and object**
>
> **We can use a relative clause to join sentences.**
>
> Read the article. The article's in the newspaper.
> Read the article **that**'s in the newspaper. (subject)
>
> Where are the things? You bought the things.
> Where are the things **that** you bought? (object)

5a **Join the sentences. Use *that*.**

1 This is the TV that isn't working.

1 This is the TV. The TV isn't working.
2 Save the files. You need the files.
3 This is the car. I want to buy the car.
4 This is the icon. You click on the icon.
5 He's the man. I saw the man yesterday.
6 She's the woman. The woman phoned.

b **Change the sentences. Use *who* or *which*.**

6a **Your life** **Write down these things.**

1 someone who you admire
2 a kind of food which you really like
3 a film that you've seen recently
4 something that you really want to do
5 a book that you want to read
6 a person who has changed your life

b **Compare your ideas with a partner.**

 Now I can ... *give further information about people and things.*

1 `71.1` **Read and listen. Why do people use Internet dating? Tick ✓ the reasons mentioned.**

– You meet people from other countries.
– You meet a lot of people.
– You always see a photograph of the person.
– You learn something about the person before you meet.

❤️ # Love online

The Internet is changing our love lives. Millions of single men and women now find a date online.

Websites aren't all the same, so you must choose the website that's best for you. A site that has a lot of young city professionals won't be very good for a middle-aged person who lives in the suburbs and likes gardening.

When you've chosen your website, you must write a good profile of yourself. Here are some ideas that can help:

1 Attach a photograph. A lot of people, especially men, won't click on a profile that hasn't got a photograph. Don't use a photo that's over five years old, and don't use one that shows you:
  – in sunglasses
  – in a swimsuit
  – or with an ex-partner.

2 Be honest. Don't say that you're a tall, handsome businessman if you're a short, ordinary-looking guy who works in an office. If you do, your first date will probably be your last.

3 Be exact. You'll find someone who likes the same things more easily. Don't write: 'I like going to the cinema.' Everybody does. Write about films that you like or a film that you've seen recently.

4 Be positive. People don't want to read about the things that you don't like. Write about the things, people, and places that you <u>do</u> like.

People use the Internet because they can meet thousands of people. They can also learn something about the other person before they meet. Will the Internet find your Mr or Ms Right?

2 **Match the reasons with the advice.**

1 Choose the right website, because …
2 Attach a photograph, because …
3 Be honest, because …
4 Be exact, because …
5 Be positive, because …

a some people won't read your profile if you don't.
b if not, you might not get another date.
c they are all different.
d people prefer reading about things that you like.
e you're more likely to find someone who has similar interests.

3 **Read these Internet dating entries. What mistakes are these people making?**

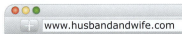

www.husbandandwife.com

1 I hate going to parties and I can't stand people who talk a lot.

2 I love listening to music and watching TV.

3 I drive a Ferrari and I often have lunch with Madonna.

4 Hi. My name's Fiona and I love sport. (No photo attached.)

5 I'm not looking for someone who wants to get married.

6 Here's a photo of me with my ex-wife.

4 `Your life` **Write your profile. Use the model below. Change the words in bold.**

I'm **Owen**. I'm **35** and I'm from **Cardiff** in **South Wales**. I'm **a psychologist** and I work in **a hospital**. I'm **medium height** and **quite slim**. I've got **blue eyes and blond hair**. I like **walking**. Most weekends I **go walking in the mountains**. I like people who **are active and sporty**. I'm looking for someone who **wants to share my outdoor activities**.

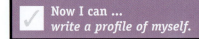
Now I can …
write a profile of myself.

1 72.1 **Read and listen.**

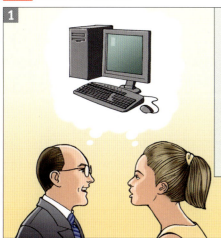

A On a computer, what do you call the thing which you look at?
B The screen.
A Screen? How do you spell that?
B It's S-C-R-double E-N.
A Oh, OK. Thanks.

A What's a plumber?
B A plumber. You don't pronounce the B.
A Oh, I see. What's a plumber?
B It's someone who fixes showers and water pipes and things like that.
A Oh, thank you.

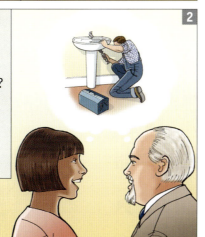

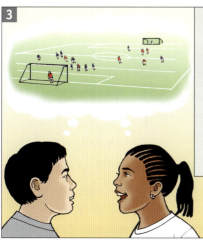

A What do you call the place where you play football?
B Do you mean a stadium?
A No, the thing that the players play on.
B Oh, the pitch. It's a football pitch.
A Thank you.

2 **Complete the expressions with these words.**

mean	what	call	how

Everyday expressions Asking what things are called

What do you _____ ... ? _____ do you spell that?
_____'s a plumber? Do you _____ a stadium?

3 72.2 **Listen. Katrin is staying in England. Choose the correct answers.**

1 What does she want?
  a a plug
  b an adaptor
  c a hairdryer
2 What does her brother do?
  a a salesman
  b a builder
  c a civil engineer
3 What does she ask about?
  a keys
  b a screensaver
  c a keyboard

Language note **Definitions**

It's someone **who** / **that** fixes showers.
It's something **which** / **that** you eat.
It's a place **where** you play football.

4a **Speaking** **Choose an example of each one of these:**
 – a job
 – a place
 – something in a kitchen
 – something that you wear
 – a family relation
 – an electrical appliance.

b **Describe the things to a partner. He / She must guess what it is.**

A *What do you call someone who cooks?*
B *Do you mean a cook?*
A *No. This is someone who works ...*

Pronunciation
/s/ or /z/

1 72.3 **Listen.**

/s/	/z/
person	choose

2a **Put the words in the correct column.**
possible thousand cursor
salesman positive website
screensaver businessman

b 72.4 **Listen, check, and repeat.**

✓ **Now I can ...** *ask about things that I don't know the name of.*

1 **73.1** Listen and repeat.

1 turn up   2 turn down

3 go away   4 come back

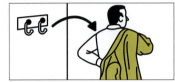 

5 put on   6 take off

7 come in   8 go out

 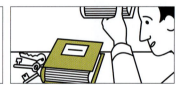

9 try on   10 look for

11 look after   12 break down

13 get up   14 throw away

 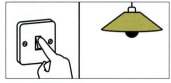

15 switch on   16 switch off

2 **73.2** Drill. Listen. Say the opposite.

1 Turn up the TV.
No. Turn down the TV.

3 Read the examples. Study the rules on page 113.

Language note Phrasal verbs

1

verb	particle
get	up
come	in

2 With some verbs the two parts show the meaning.

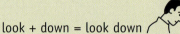

look + up = look up

look + down = look down

look + back = look back

3 With some verbs you can't see the meaning from the two parts.

look after   break down

4 **73.3** Listen. There are two verbs in each conversation. Number them.

look after ___   go out ___
switch off ___   sit down *1*
stand up ___   look for ___
put on ___   go away ___
come in *1*   switch on ___

5 **Your life** Ask and answer with a partner.

1 What time do you get up at weekends?
2 How often do you go out with your friends?
3 Do you look after anyone?
4 What do you take off first when you get home?
5 What was the last thing that you threw away?
6 What things do you often have to look for?
7 What time do you normally switch off the TV in the evening?
8 What clothes do you always try on before you buy them?

✓ **Now I can ...**
use some common phrasal verbs.

1 [74.1] Read and listen.

Lucy is at a conference. She's met an old friend from college.

Lucy Lovely to see you again, Alma. I **haven't seen** you since your 21st birthday party. Do you still live in London?

Alma No, I don't. I lived here for a few years after college, but then I moved to York.

Lucy Are you married?

Alma Yes, I am. I**'ve been** married **since** last February.

Lucy Congratulations. How long **have** you **lived** in York?

Alma Oh, I**'ve lived** there **for** nearly three years now.

Lucy Do you remember that guy who was studying Engineering? Oh, what was his name? Ben Driver. Wasn't he from York?

Alma Yes, he was. I ...

Lucy He was so boring! I **haven't seen** him since we left college.

Alma I have. I saw him this morning actually. He's my husband!

2 Read the examples. Study the rules on page 113.

Present perfect: *for* and *since*

1 I**'ve lived** there for six years. = I still live there now.
I **lived** there for five years. = I don't live there now.

2 *for* + a period of time   **for** three years
since + a point of time   **since** last February

3 Write *for* or *since*.

1 We've been here *since* yesterday.
2 I've worked here _____ two weeks.
3 They've been married _____ 1995.
4 We haven't seen each other _____ ages.
5 She's been away _____ five days.
6 I've had a headache _____ this morning.

4 Put the verbs in brackets into the present perfect or past simple.

1 I *'ve been* at work since eight o'clock, but I'm going to leave soon. (be)
2 We _____ on holiday last week. (be)
3 I _____ at the restaurant for an hour, but then I left. (wait)
4 We must get a new car. We _____ this one for ten years. (have)
5 I'm a vegetarian. I _____ meat since I was a teenager. (not eat)
6 I _____ for nearly twenty years, but I stopped last year. (smoke)

5 [74.2] Listen. Tick ✓ the correct sentence.

1 a She works there now. ✓
  b She doesn't work there now.
2 a He's a policeman.
  b He isn't a policeman.
3 a They're married.
  b They aren't married.
4 a They still live in France.
  b They don't live in France now.
5 a She works at the bank.
  b She doesn't work at the bank.

6 Writing Complete the sentences.

1 I live in _____.
2 I've lived there for / since _____.
3 I'm a _____ (*job*).
4 I've been a _____ for / since _____.
5 I work / study in / at _____.
6 I've worked / studied there for / since _____.
7 In my free time, I _____.
8 I've played / done for / since _____.
9 My parents have been / were married for / since _____.

Pronunciation
Vowel sounds

[74.3] Listen. Choose the odd one out.
1 down   out   throw
2 back   take   break
3 look   up   put
4 there   here   year
5 was   saw   off
6 find   sit   since
7 turn   work   fork
8 won   gone   done

✓ **Now I can ...** *talk about past activities that continue to the present.*

1 **75.1** **Listen. Paul and Helen are at a university reunion. Answer the questions.**

1 Which person ...
– has worked for the same company since university?
– has had a lot of different jobs?
2 Who are Troy and Georgina?

> **Paul:** Helen, it's good to see you.

> **Helen:** Yes, and you, Paul. How are you?

2a **Write Paul (P) or Helen (H).**

1 _H_ is divorced.
2 _P_ is married.
3 ____ has travelled a lot.
4 ____ has got three children.
5 ____ lives in Manchester.
6 ____ worked for an insurance company.
7 ____ lives in London.
8 ____ shares a flat with a friend.
9 ____ lives in a house in the suburbs.
10 ____ works for a computer company.
11 ____ works for a bank.
12 ____ was a singer in a band.

b **Listen again. Check your ideas.**

3a **Paul and Helen mention these periods of time. Why?**
– six months
– a couple of years
– three years
– four years
– nine years

b **Listen again. Check your ideas.**

4 **What do Paul and Helen think about each other's life?**

5a **Speaking** **You've met an old friend after 15 years. Think about your answers to these questions.**

1 What do you do?
2 How long have you been a ... ?
3 Where do you live / work?
4 How long have you lived / worked there?
5 Where did you live / work before?
6 How long did you live / work there?
7 Are you married?
8 How long have you been married?
9 Have you got any children?
10 What do you do in your free time?
11 How long have you done ... / played ... ?

b **Work with a partner. Make the conversation. Use the questions.**

English in the world
Reunions

Universities and some schools in Britain and the USA usually have reunions for their former students. They often have a magazine, too, with news of former students' lives.
Reunions are big events in the USA. They are normally used to raise money for the university or school.
Now there are websites, too, where people can find old friends.

Compare this with your country.

 Now I can ...
talk about my life up to now.

1 Look back at Episodes 8 and 9. What happened?

2 `76.1` **Read and listen to the story.**

  1 Where are Ryan and Cindy going? Why?

  2 Does Sarah speak to Ryan or Cindy?

3 Are the statements true (T) or false (F)?

  1 Russell hasn't put any petrol in the car.

  2 Someone answers the phone at The Coffee Shop.

  3 Russell is using Ryan's mobile.

  4 Cindy hasn't got her mobile with her.

  5 Russell knows the solicitor's name.

  6 The solicitor's office isn't near the café.

  7 Anna Harlow is at The Coffee Shop.

  8 Russell saw Anna three days ago.

4a Complete the expressions.

> **Everyday expressions** Telephoning
>
> There's _____ reply.
> I'll _____ his mobile.
> It_____ ringing.
> She hasn't got her phone _____ her.
> It's re-_____.
> Don't hang _____.

b Complete the sentences. Use the expressions.

  1 Oh, wait, one more thing … just a minute – _____.

  2 I can't phone her, because _____.

  3 There's no reply from his office, so _____.

  4 _____, but nobody's answering it.

  5 I've tried to phone them, but _____.

  6 I haven't got my mobile with me because _____.

5 Language check. <u>Underline</u> examples of the present perfect in the story.

6 Work in a group. Practise the story.

Ryan Oh no! Russell hasn't put any petrol in the car again! We haven't used it since Monday and it's nearly empty.

Cindy Well, we can get some petrol on the way.

Peter There's no reply at The Coffee Shop.

Sarah I'll try Ryan's mobile. … It's ringing. Hello, Ryan. It's Sarah. I …

Russell Hi, Sarah. This is Russell. I've borrowed Dad's mobile.

Sarah Oh, well. Is your dad there?

Russell No. Mum and Dad have gone to the solicitor's. They're going to sign the contract to sell this place.

Sarah Oh, OK. I'll try your mum's mobile.

Russell Actually, she hasn't got her phone with her. It's re-charging here.

Sarah Oh, no! … Oh, don't hang up, Russell! Here's Jordan.

Jordan Russell, do you know the name of your parents' solicitor?

Russell No, sorry, but it isn't near here, because they've gone in the car.

Jordan What about Anna? Is she there?

Russell Anna? No, I haven't seen her for two weeks. Look. I must go. There are customers in the café. Bye.

It's too late. They're going to sell The Coffee Shop!

Now I can …
talk about telephoning.

1 `77.1` **Listen and repeat.**

1 tired

2 hungry

3 thirsty

4 bored

5 interested

6 worried

7 annoyed

8 excited

9 relaxed

10 embarrassed

11 frightened

12 surprised

13 confused

14 miserable

15 proud

2a `77.2` **Listen. How does Mark feel each time?**

1 worried

b Listen again. Match the reasons with the feelings from exercise 2a.

1 worried – d

a There's nothing on TV.
b He was at a party last night.
c He's had a day off.
d He's got an interview tomorrow.
e He's not sure about the meeting date.
f His son won a school prize.
g He didn't have any lunch.
h His laptop isn't working.

> **Language note** *-ed / -ing* adjectives
>
> I don't like this film. I'm **bored**.
> The film is **boring**.
>
> I like this book. I'm **interested**.
> The book is **interesting**.

3 Choose the correct words to complete the sentences.

1 There's a very *interested / interesting* article in the newspaper today.
2 I'm *bored / boring*. I've got nothing to do.
3 You should go to bed. You look *tired / tiring*.
4 That's very *annoyed / annoying*. There's a car in my parking space.
5 This horror film is *frightened / frightening*.
6 I forgot the Managing Director's name. It was very *embarrassed / embarrassing*.
7 He's *excited / exciting*. He's got a new job.
8 I don't understand these instructions. They're very *confused / confusing*.

4a `Your life` **Give an example of a person, place, or thing for each of these words.**

1 I think sport is interesting.

1 interesting	5 exciting
2 boring	6 frightening
3 annoying	7 confusing
4 relaxing	8 surprising

b Compare your ideas with a partner.

5 Write six sentences about yourself.

I feel/felt embarrassed when ...

 Now I can ...
talk about feelings.

1 `78.1` **Read and listen.**

FIRE! Save my wallet!

If your house **was** on fire, you**'d get out** quickly. However, you**'d** probably **take** some things, too. What **would you take** with you? An insurance company asked people this question. Most men, it seems, **would look for** something valuable, like their wallet, computer, or CD collection.

Most women, however, would save personal things. 'I **wouldn't save** my purse,' said one woman. 'You can replace things like that. I'd take things that you can't buy like family photographs. I'd save a pet first if we **had** one.'

2 **Read the examples. Study the rules on page 114.**

> **would + verb**
>
> **1** We use the conditional form with *would* for imaginary or unlikely events.
>
> **2** Most people **would get out** quickly.
> I**'d save** the pet.
> Most women **would not take** the TV.
> He **wouldn't take** the family photos.
>
> **3** **Would** you **save** your credit cards? Yes, I **would**.
> No, I **wouldn't**.
>
> Why **would** you **take** that?

3a **What would you save? Choose your top five things.**

I'd save my books. OR *I wouldn't save a computer.*

– books	– documents and certificates
– a pet	– your wallet or purse
– a computer	– a CD collection
– jewellery	– clothes
– family photos	– your mobile phone

b **Ask and answer with a partner. Ask for reasons.**

A *Would you save your books?*
B *Yes. I would./No, I wouldn't.*
A *Why would/wouldn't you save them?*

4 **Read the examples. Study the rules on page 114.**

> **Second conditional**
>
> **1** We use *would* in a second conditional sentence for imaginary or unreal conditions.
> If their house **was** on fire, most people **would get out** quickly.
> OR
> Most people **would get out** quickly if their house **was** on fire.
>
> **2** We use:
> – the past simple in the *if* clause.
> – the conditional with *would* in the main clause.
> NOT ~~If their house would be on fire, most people would get out quickly.~~

5 **Put the verbs in brackets in the past simple or conditional form.**

1 If I ___had___ (have) a year off, I'*d travel* (travel) round the world.
2 If I _____ (find) a mobile phone, I _____ (not use) it.
3 I _____ (learn) another language if I _____ (have) more time.
4 If someone _____ (steal) my mobile phone, I _____ (contact) the police.
5 I _____ (stay) in bed if it _____ (be) Sunday today.
6 If we _____ (not have) an exam tomorrow, I _____ (come) with you.

6a **Speaking** **What would you do in these situations? Complete the sentences.**

1 If I had two extra hours a day, _____.
2 If I found someone's mobile, _____.
3 If I was the boss / headteacher, _____.
4 If I travelled back in time, _____.
5 If I had a year off, _____.

b **Ask and answer with a partner.**

A *What would you do if you had two extra hours a day?*
B *I'd …*
A *Why would you do that?*
B *Because …*

> ✓ **Now I can …**
> *talk about imaginary or unlikely events.*

1 `79.1` **Read and listen to the text. What is the answer to the question in the title?**

WHICH WOULD MAKE YOU HAPPIER – DOING THIS OR

HAVING THIS?

I f you won the lottery, what would you do with the money? Would you buy a big house, a yacht perhaps, or a fast, expensive sports car? We all dream of buying these things, but would they make us happier?

'No, they wouldn't,' says Rupert Sweeney. He works for a large bank and has studied the psychology of money. 'If you bought a new sports car', he says, 'it would be good at first. Then after a while it wouldn't be new and interesting. It would become normal. So then what would you do? You'd want a faster car or a more expensive one. So in the end your nice sports car would make you unhappy, because you'd always want something better.'

Material things like cars, watches, houses, and clothes only make you happy for a while. We're all a lot richer than we were in the 1950s, but we aren't happier. The things that will really make you happy are:
– doing things that you enjoy and;
– spending time with people that you like.

If you won a lot of money, what should you spend it on then? 'Experiences,' says Rupert Sweeney. 'Learn something new, like water-skiing. Do something that you've always wanted to do. Eat at a five-star restaurant. Visit places that you've never been to. Every experience is special, and experiences get better with time, because we forget the bad things in life. And if you share the experiences with your family and friends, you'll enjoy them again and again with photos, videos, and memories.'

So, if that big cheque ever arrives, forget the fast car and the designer clothes. Book those skydiving lessons for yourself and your friends.

2 **Answer the questions.**
1 Where does Rupert Sweeney work?
2 What has he studied?
3 Why do material things only make us happy for a while?
4 What are the things that really make us happy?
5 Why do experiences get better with time?
6 How can you enjoy experiences again and again?

3 **What examples does the article give of ... ?**
– material things
– experiences

Language note	Time expressions
at first	in the end
then	for a (short) while
after a while	again and again

4 **Do you agree with the writer? Why? Why not?**

5 Your life **Work with a partner. Discuss these questions.**

If you won a lot of money, ...
– what things would you buy?
– what activities would you do?
– what new things would you learn?
– what places would you visit?

Who would you do these things with?
Why would you do these things?

Pronunciation
How many syllables?

1 `79.2` **Listen. How many syllables are there: 1, 2, 3, or 4?**

relaxed interesting psychology bored
material worried tired embarrassed
frightened experience miserable clothes

2 `79.3` **Listen, check, and repeat.**

✓	Now I can ...
	talk about things that I'd like to do.

1 **80.1** Read and listen.

1

18 July

Dear Victoria

Just a note to say thank you for the lovely birthday card and present that you sent. I started the book yesterday and it's very exciting.

I hope you're well.

Love,

Charlotte

2

To: sandrasif36@abc.com
Subject: Thank you

Dear Sandra and Asif

I'm just writing to say thank you for the great party at your place on Saturday. I really enjoyed the evening. The food was delicious and I met some very interesting people.

Hope to see you soon.

All the best,

Mack

2 **Read the notes again. Answer the questions.**

1 Who had a birthday recently?
2 Who sent her a present?
3 What else did she send?
4 What was the present?
5 Who went to a party?
6 Where was the party?
7 When was it?
8 Was there any food at the party?

3 **What do the people describe with these words?**

1 lovely
2 exciting
3 great
4 delicious
5 interesting

4 **Complete the expressions.**

Everyday expressions
Saying thank you

Introduction
Just a _____ to say ...
I'm just _____ to say ...
Message
Thank you _____ dinner/the present.
Ending
I hope you're _____.
Hope to see _____ soon.
Signing off
Love,
All _____ best,
Best wishes,

5 **Complete the thank-you note.**

¹_____ Mario and Silvia
I ²_____ to ³_____
the very nice weekend that I spent with you and your family in Milan. I ⁴_____ the weekend, and thought your house was beautiful.
I hope ⁵_____.

All ⁶_____

Andy

6 **Writing** Write thank-you notes/emails for these situations:

– a friend took you for lunch last week
– someone sent you a CD for your birthday.

English in the world
Parties

At a party in an English-speaking country, the hosts normally provide drinks, but guests often bring a bottle of wine, too. There are usually snacks, such as peanuts and crisps. Sometimes there is food, too. It's normally a buffet. People usually stand up at parties in small groups.

Now I can ...
✓ *write a thank-you note.*

1   **Look back at Episode 10. What happened?**

2   **81.1** **Read and listen to the story.**

3a **What do you think happened at the solicitor's?**

b   **81.2** **Listen and check your ideas.**

1

Lucy	Hi, everyone!
Jordan	Hello, Lucy. You're early.
Lucy	Yes. I had the afternoon off. Hey. What's wrong? Why is everyone so sad?
Peter	Sit down, Lucy. We'll tell you all about it.

2 *Later…*

Jordan	So Ryan and Cindy have gone to the solicitor's to sell The Coffee Shop.
Lucy	Well, why didn't you phone me? I know their solicitor. The phone number's on the board over there.
Sarah	Come on, then. Let's phone them.
Peter	But it's already ten past five. They've probably gone home now.
Lucy	Yes, you're right. There's no reply.

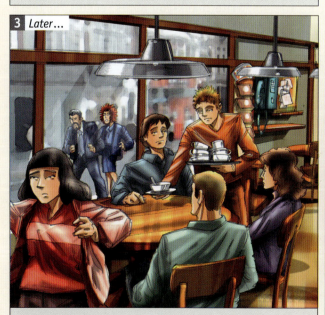

3 *Later…*

Peter	Would anyone like another cup of coffee?
Sarah	Not for me, thanks. I must go.
Lucy	Oh, just a minute. Here are Ryan and Cindy.
Jordan	They don't look very happy.

4

Ryan	Where's that stupid boy? I'll kill him!
Cindy	Calm down, Ryan.
Ryan	Calm down? It's all his fault!
Russell	Hi, Mum, Dad. Look. I'm really sorry. I didn't know.
Sarah	It's true, Ryan. Russell didn't know anything about Anna and Starlight Properties.

Now I can …
start **English for Life** *Intermediate.*

STUDY AND REFERENCE SECTION
Contents

Review 1–8

Vocabulary

1 Complete the conversation.

there	where	Japan	pleased
from	know	in	~~name's~~

A Hi, my [1] *name's* Mika.
B [2] _____ to meet you, Mika. I'm Jorge.
A [3] _____ are you from, Jorge?
B I'm [4] _____ Argentina. And you?
A I'm from [5] _____.
B Oh, really? Whereabouts [6] _____ Japan?
A Osaka. Do you [7] _____ it?
B Yes, I do. I was [8] _____ last year.

2 Write four jobs and four work places.

Jobs	Places
a nurse	*a salon*

3 Match the sentence halves.

1 Gardeners work __   a a uniform.
2 He wears __   b a computer.
3 We do shift __   c work.
4 I use __   d outdoors.

Grammar

4a Put the words in the correct order to make questions.

1 Where were you born?
1 were you where born ?
2 what name your 's ?
3 live in London you do ?
4 you got have a brother ?
5 you single are ?

b Answer the questions.

5a Complete the sentences. Use the present simple form of the verbs in brackets.

1 I _live_ near the school. (live)
2 They _____ in a factory. (work)
3 She _____ him. (like)
4 He _____ two sisters. (have got)
5 We usually _____ work at 9 a.m. (start)

b Make the sentences negative.

1 I don't live near the school.

Skills

6a Read the text and complete the form.

My name's Omar Hamedi and I'm from Egypt. I'm an engineer in Cairo and my wife is a doctor. We've got three children.

1 Title: _Mr_	5 Occupation: _____
2 First name: _____	6 Marital status: _____
3 Surname: _____	7 No. of dependants: _____
4 Nationality: _____	

b Copy the form. Write your personal details.

7 Read the text. Tick ✓ or correct the sentences.

Brigitta Pataki is Hungarian. She works at a radio station in Canada. She starts work at 4.00 p.m. and finishes at 12.00 p.m. Brigitta likes her job, but there are some problems. She works six days a week and she can never go out in the evening.

1 Brigitta is from Hungary.
1 Brigitta is from Canada.
2 She works at a radio station.
3 She works in the morning.
4 Her shift is eight hours.
5 She has two days off a week.

English for Everyday Life

8 Choose the correct word.

1 How *are / is* you?
2 Are you busy *in / at* the moment?
3 How *are / is* Marco?
4 *Is / Are* he busy?

9 Write the missing months.

January, _____, March, _____, May, _____, July, _____, September, _____, November, _____

10 Complete the conversation.

A [1]*Hello*, Mill Dental Practice.
B Hello, I've got an appointment [2]o_ 4 May.
A What [3]t___ is your appointment?
B It's at 4.30, but I'm afraid I [4]c__'_ make it.
A Would you like to [5]m___ another appointment?
B Yes, [6]p_____.
A Can you [7]c___ on 7 May at 3.30?
B Yes, that's [8]f___.

1 country /ˈkʌntri/
Brazil (n) /brəˈzɪl/
Canada (n) /ˈkænədə/
Italy (n) /ˈɪtəli/
Poland (n) /ˈpəʊlənd/
nationality /ˌnæʃəˈnæləti/
American (adj) /əˈmerɪˌkən/
Brazilian (adj) /brəˈzɪliən/
Canadian (adj) /kəˈneɪdiən/
Chinese (adj) /ˌtʃaɪˈniːz/
Egyptian (adj) /iˈdʒɪpʃn/
French (adj) /frentʃ/
Greek (adj) /griːk/
Irish (adj) /ˈaɪrɪʃ/
Japanese (adj) /dʒæpəˈniːz/
Polish (adj) /ˈpəʊlɪʃ/
Russian (adj) /ˈrʌʃn/
Spanish (adj) /ˈspænɪʃ/
I'm from ... (exp) /aɪm frəm/
My name's ... (exp) /maɪ neɪmz/
whereabouts (adv) /ˌweərəˈbaʊts/

2 be born (v) /bi ˈbɔːn/
birthday (n) /ˈbɜːθdeɪ/
free time (n) /ˌfri ˈtaɪm/
last name (n) /laːst neɪm/
live (v) /lɪv/
married (adj) /ˈmærɪd/
near (prep) /nɪə(r)/

3 personal details (n) /ˈpɜːsənl ˌdiːteɪlz/
surname (n) /ˈsɜːneɪm/
title (n) /ˈtaɪtl/
marital status (n) /ˈmærɪtl ˌsteɪtəs/
divorced (adj) /dɪˈvɔːst/
single (adj) /ˈsɪŋgl/
separated (adj) /ˈsepəreɪtɪd/
widowed (adj) /ˈwɪdəʊd/
gender (n) /ˈdʒendə(r)/
female (adj) /ˈfiːmeɪl/
male (adj) /meɪl/
date of birth (n) /deɪt əv ˈbɜːθ/
dependant (n) /dɪˈpendənt/
no. (abbrev = number) /ˈnʌmbər/
occupation (n) /ˌɒkjuˈpeɪʃn/
contact details (n) /ˈkɒntækt ˌdiːteɪlz/

4 at the moment (adv) /æt ðə ˈməʊmənt/
busy (adj) /ˈbɪzi/
these days (exp) /ˈðiːz deɪz/
actor (n) /ˈæktə(r)/
advertising agency (n) /ˈædvətaɪzɪŋ ˌeɪdʒ(ə)nsi/
computer engineer (n) /kəmˈpjuːtə(r) ˌendʒɪnˈɪə(r)/
magazine company (n) /ˌmægəˈziːn ˌkʌmpəni/
personal assistant (n) /ˈpɜːsənl əˈsɪst(ə)nt/

5 artist (n) /ˈɑːtɪst/
electrician (n) /ɪˌlekˈtrɪʃn/
flight attendant (n) /ˈflaɪt əˌtendənt/
gardener (n) /ˈgɑːdnə(r)/
hairdresser (n) /ˈheədresə(r)/
lorry driver (n) /ˈlɒri ˌdraɪvə(r)/
plumber (n) /ˈplʌmə(r)/
police officer (n) /pəˈliːs ˌɒfɪsə(r)/
factory (n) /ˈfæktri/
hotel (n) /həʊˈtel/
studio (n) /ˈstjuːdiəʊ/
salon (n) /ˈsælɒn/
do shift work (v) /ˌduː ˈʃɪft ˌwɜːk/
look after people (v) /ˌlʊk ˈɑːftə ˌpiːpl/
repair things (v) /rɪˈpeə(r) ˌθɪŋz/
use a computer (v) /juːz ə kəmˈpjuːtə(r)/
wear a uniform (v) /ˌweə(r) ə ˈjuːnɪˌfɔːm/
work outdoors (v) /ˌwɜːk aʊtˈdɔːz/

6 at night (adv) /æt naɪt/
during the day (adv) /ˌdjʊərɪŋ ðə ˈdeɪ/
every day (adv) /ˌevri ˈdeɪ/
normally (adv) /ˈnɔːməli/
often (adv) /ˈɒfn/
usually (adv) /ˈjuːʒuəli/
finish work (v) /ˌfɪnɪʃ ˈwɜːk/
get home (v) /ˌget ˈhəʊm/
go to bed (v) /ˌgəʊ tə ˈbed/
gorgeous (adj) /ˈgɔːdʒəs/
have a meal (v) /ˌhæv ə ˈmiːl/
old people's home (n) /ˌəʊld ˈpiːplz ˌhəʊm/
start work (v) /ˌstɑːt ˈwɜːk/
What does she do? (exp) /ˌwɒt dʌz ʃi ˈduː/

7 all the time (adv) /ˌɔːl ðə ˈtaɪm/
always (adv) /ˈɔːlweɪz/
never (adv) /ˈnevə(r)/
rarely (adv) /ˈreəli/
sometimes (adv) /ˈsʌmtaɪmz/
electrical engineer (n) /ɪˌlektrɪkl endʒɪnˈɪə(r)/
workplace (n) /ˈwɜːkpleɪs/
oil rig (n) /ˈɔɪl rɪg/
power station (n) /ˈpaʊə(r) ˌsteɪʃn/
day shift (n) /ˈdeɪ ʃɪft/
get seasick (v) /ˌget ˈsiːsɪk/
night shift (n) /ˈnaɪt ʃɪft/
on duty /ɒn ˈdjuːti/
telephone banking (n) /ˈtelɪfəʊn ˌbæŋkɪŋ/
working hours (n pl) /ˈwɜːkɪŋ aʊəz/

8 I can't make that. (exp) /aɪ kɑːnt ˈmeɪk ðæt/
afternoon (n) /ˌɑːftəˈnuːn/
appointment (n) /əˈpɔɪntmənt/
dental practice (n) /ˈdentl ˌpræktɪs/
interview (n) /ˈɪntəvjuː/

Review 9–16

Vocabulary

1 Choose the correct verb for each collocation.

1 They *go* / *make* shopping on Sunday.
2 I *do* / *have* a shower in the evening.
3 He always *goes* / *gets* up at 6.50 a.m.
4 We *do* / *make* the housework on Sunday.
5 She usually *has* / *does* a rest in the afternoon.

2 Complete the sentences.

| got married | met | grew up |
| died | ~~was born~~ | had |

1 Elvis Presley _was born_ in 1935.
2 He _____ in Mississippi in the USA.
3 He _____ his future wife in Germany.
4 They _____ on 1 May 1967.
5 They _____ a daughter called Lisa Marie.
6 He _____ in 1977, aged 42.

Grammar

3 Write the past simple of the verbs.

1 go _went_
2 hurry _____
3 stop _____
4 leave _____
5 be _____
6 have _____
7 arrive _____
8 put _____

4a Make sentences with the past simple. Use the cues.

1 Yesterday was a good day for Julio.

1 Yesterday / be / a good day for Julio.
2 He / meet / his friends for lunch.
3 His boss / be / away.
4 He / go / home early.
5 His noisy neighbours / be / away.
6 He / watch / a football match on TV.

b Make the sentences negative.

Yesterday wasn't a good day for Julio.

5a Put the words in the correct order to make questions.

1 Where did you go yesterday?

1 Where you did yesterday go ?
2 you speak to Who did ?
3 you Were at work ?
4 you Did on go a date ?
5 time you What did to bed go ?

b Answer the questions. Say what you did yesterday.

Skills

6 Read the text. Answer the questions.

Hans and Ilse Braun lived in Berlin. Hans had a good job in a bank and Ilsa was a French teacher. However, they weren't happy because they worked long hours and didn't spend much time together. In 2003 they decided to change their lives. They sold their house and bought a language school in France. Now Ilsa teaches German and Hans writes books. They live in a flat near the school and are very happy.

1 Where did Hans and Ilse live?
2 Where did Hans work?
3 Why were they unhappy?
4 When did they decide to change their lives?
5 Which country did they move to?
6 What does Ilse do now?

English for Everyday Life

7 Match the halves of the expressions.

1 That's ___   a really?
2 Oh, ___   b you mean.
3 I heard ___   c true.
4 I see what ___   d about that.

8 Complete the conversations.

| news | done | congratulations | ~~go~~ | luck |

1 A How did Jaime's exam _go_ ?
  B He passed.
2 A I got the job.
  B Well _____!
3 A We lost the football match.
  B Better _____ next time.
4 A I won £1,000.
  B That's fantastic _____!
5 A We got married last week.
  B _____!

Wordlist 9–16

9 | do homework (v) | /ˌduː ˈhəʊmwɜːk/
 | do housework (v) | /ˌduː ˈhaʊswɜːk/
 | do the ironing (v) | /ˌduː ði ˈaɪənɪŋ/
 | get up (v) | /ˌget ˈʌp/
 | get home (v) | /ˌget ˈhəʊm/
 | get dressed (v) | /ˌget ˈdrest/
 | go out (v) | /ˌgəʊ ˈaʊt/
 | go shopping (v) | /ˌgəʊ ˈʃɒpɪŋ/
 | go to bed (v) | /ˌgəʊ tə ˈbed/
 | have a rest (v) | /ˌhæv ə ˈrest/
 | have a shower (v) | /ˌhæv ə ˈʃaʊə(r)/
 | have breakfast (v) | /ˌhæv ˈbrekfəst/
 | make a cup of coffee (v) | /ˌmeɪk ə kʌp əv ˈkɒfi/
 | make an appointment (v) | /ˌmeɪk ən əˈpɔɪntmənt/
 | make the bed (v) | /ˌmeɪk ðə ˈbed/

10 | bill (n) | /bɪl/
 | drop (v) | /drɒp/
 | go wrong (v) | /ˌgəʊ ˈrɒŋ/
 | hall (n) | /hɔːl/
 | hurry (v) | /ˈhʌri/
 | in a hurry (exp) | /ˌɪn ə ˈhʌri/
 | late (adj) | /leɪt/
 | meeting (n) | /ˈmiːtɪŋ/
 | neighbour (n) | /ˈneɪbə(r)/
 | on time (exp) | /ˌɒn ˈtaɪm/
 | pocket (n) | /ˈpɒkɪt/
 | post (n) | /pəʊst/
 | queue (n) | /kjuː/

11 | argument (n) | /ˈɑːgjumənt/
 | contract (n) | /ˈkɒntrækt/
 | deal with (v) | /ˈdiːl wɪð/
 | earn (v) | /ɜːn/
 | estate agent (n) | /ɪˈsteɪt ˌeɪdʒ(ə)nt/
 | legal matter (n) | /ˈliːgl ˌmætə(r)/
 | mortgage (n) | /ˈmɔːgɪdʒ/
 | move house (v) | /ˌmuːv ˈhaʊs/
 | own (v) | /əʊn/
 | solicitor (n) | /səˈlɪsɪtə/
 | take out (v) | /ˌteɪk ˈaʊt/

12 | I heard about that. (exp) | /aɪ ˈhɜːd əbaʊt ˌðæt/
 | I see what you mean. (exp) | /aɪ ˌsiː wɒt juː ˈmiːn/
 | Oh, I see. (exp) | /ˌəʊ aɪ ˈsiː/
 | Oh, right. (exp) | /ˌəʊ ˈraɪt/
 | That's true. (exp) | /ˈðæts ˌtruː/
 | make money (v) | /ˌmeɪk ˈmʌni/
 | lose money (v) | /ˌluːz ˈmʌni/
 | save money (v) | /ˌseɪv ˈmʌni/
 | close down (v) | /ˌkləʊz ˈdaʊn/
 | eat like a horse (exp) | /ˌiːt laɪk ə ˈhɔːs/
 | look good (exp) | /ˌlʊk ˈgʊd/
 | till (prep) | /tɪl/

13 | be born (v) | /biː ˈbɔːn/
 | die (v) | /daɪ/
 | fall in love (v) | /ˌfɔːl ɪn ˈlʌv/
 | get a job (v) | /ˌget ə ˈdʒɒb/
 | get divorced (v) | /ˌget dɪˈvɔːst/
 | get married (v) | /ˌget ˈmærid/
 | go out with (v) | /ˌgəʊ ˈaʊt wɪð/
 | graduate (v) | /ˈgrædʒueɪt/
 | grow up (v) | /ˌgrəʊ ˈʌp/
 | have children (v) | /ˌhæv ˈtʃɪldrən/
 | lose a job (v) | /ˌluːz ə ˈdʒɒb/
 | meet your future husband/wife (v) | /ˌmiːt jɔː(r) ˌfjuːtʃə ˈhʌzbənd ɔː ˈwaɪf/
 | move house (v) | /ˌmuːv ˈhaʊs/
 | retire (v) | /rɪˈtaɪə(r)/
 | take an exam (v) | /ˌteɪk ən ɪgˈzæm/

14 | anyway (adv) | /ˈeniweɪ/
 | child (n) | /tʃaɪld/
 | how (adv) | /haʊ/
 | go on a date (v) | /ˌgəʊ ɒn ə ˈdeɪt/
 | guy (n) | /gaɪ/
 | later (adj) | /ˈleɪtə(r)/
 | laugh (v) | /lɑːf/
 | leave school (v) | /ˌliːv ˈskuːl/
 | on business (exp) | /ˌɒn ˈbɪznəs/
 | subject (n) | /ˈsʌbdʒɪkt/
 | tour guide (n) | /ˈtʊə(r) ˌgaɪd/
 | wedding (n) | /ˈwedɪŋ/
 | well (exp) | /wel/

15 | blues (n) | /bluːz/
 | classical music (n) | /ˈklæsɪkəl ˌmjuːzɪk/
 | country music (n) | /ˈkʌntri ˌmjuːzɪk/
 | gospel (n) | /ˈgɒspl/
 | jazz (n) | /dʒæz/
 | soul (n) | /səʊl/
 | create (v) | /kriˈeɪt/
 | dark (adj) | /dɑːk/
 | film director (n) | /ˈfɪlm dəˌrektə(r)/
 | go blind (v) | /ˌgəʊ ˈblaɪnd/
 | heroin (n) | /ˈherəʊɪn/
 | Oscar (n) | /ˈɒskə(r)/

16 | Congratulations! (exp) | /kənˌgrætʃuˈleɪʃnz/
 | That's fantastic news! (exp) | /ðæts fænˈtæstɪk ˌnjuːz/
 | Well done! (exp) | /ˌwel ˈdʌn/
 | I knew you could do it. (exp) | /aɪ ˌnjuː juː kəd ˌduː ɪt/
 | Never mind. (exp) | /ˈnevə ˌmaɪnd/
 | Better luck next time. (exp) | /ˈbetə lʌk ˌnekst taɪm/
 | Oh, dear. (exp) | /ˌəʊ ˈdɪə/
 | That's a pity. (exp) | /ˈðæts ə ˌpɪti/
 | How did it go? (exp) | /ˌhaʊ dɪd ɪt ˈgəʊ/

Vocabulary

1 Match the pictures with the locations and directions.

1 go round *e*
2 go down ___
3 go under ___
4 go into ___
5 go up ___
6 go out of ___
7 go through ___
8 at the top ___
9 go over ___
10 at the bottom ___

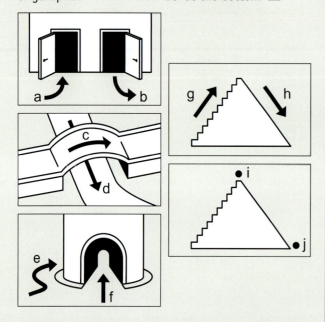

Grammar

2 Choose the correct form.

1 We usually *cycle* / *are cycling* to school.
2 You *don't work* / *aren't working* on Saturdays.
3 Pavel *has* / *'s having* lunch at the moment.
4 *Do you usually wear* / *Are you usually wearing* jeans?
5 It *doesn't snow* / *isn't snowing* today.

3 Complete the sentences. Put the verbs in the past continuous.

write	play	watch	make

1 I _____ an email.
2 Martin and Erik _____ golf.
3 Amelie _____ dinner.
4 Alexis and Mo _____ a DVD.

4 Complete the answers.

1 Were you making lunch? Yes, I _____ .
2 Were Joe and Mel working? Yes, they _____ .
3 Was In-sook writing an email? No, she _____ .
4 Were Tak Hung and Tony studying? No, they _____ .

Skills

5 Match the sentences with the responses.

1 The airport, please. *c*   a With friends.
2 Are you here on holiday? ___   b Thank you.
3 Do you like New York? ___   c Which terminal?
4 Where are you staying? ___   d Yes, it's very nice.
5 Enjoy your holiday. ___   e No, on business.

6 Read the text. Are the statements true (T) or false (F)?

My name is Javi and I'm from Spain. Last year I was in Wales for a meeting. One evening I was driving back to my hotel and I passed an old pub called The Castle Tavern. I decided to stop and have a drink. I was the only person in the pub. An old woman wearing a black dress served my drink. She said she was the owner of the pub. The next day I told the hotel receptionist about the pub. He looked very surprised. 'That's impossible,' he said. 'The Castle Tavern closed in 1957 when the owner died.'

1 Javi is Spanish. *T*
2 He was on holiday.
3 He was walking back to his hotel.
4 The pub was very busy.
5 A young woman served him.
6 The woman was wearing a black dress.
7 The Castle Tavern closed in 1957.
8 The owner is still alive.

English for Everyday Life

7 Put the words in the correct order to make expressions.

1 you like a Would hand ?
2 kind very 's That .
3 Can hand give you me a ?
4 it No, 's OK .

8 Complete the directions.

end	~~directions~~	traffic lights	hand
for	along	turn	about

Here are the [1]*directions* to our office. When you leave the motorway, [2]_____ left. Drive [3]_____ the road for [4]_____ a kilometre. Look [5]_____ a hospital on the right- [6]_____ side. Turn left at the next [7]_____. Our offices are at the [8]_____ of the street, on the corner.

Wordlist 17–24

17
change (v)	/tʃeɪndʒ/
depart from (v)	/dɪ'pɑːt ˌfrəm/
direct (adj)	/dɪ'rekt/
express (n)	/ɪk'spres/
fare (n)	/feə(r)/
first class (adj)	/ˌfɜːst 'klɑːs/
get to (v)	/'get tu/
local train (n)	/'ləʊkl ˌtreɪn/
platform (n)	/'plætfɔːm/
return (n)	/rɪ'tɜːn/
seat reservation (n)	/'siːt rezəˌveɪʃn/
single (n)	/'sɪŋgl/
standard class (n)	/'stændəd ˌklɑːs/
station (n)	/'steɪʃn/
train (n)	/treɪn/

18
cycle (v)	/'saɪkl/
do a crossword (v)	/ˌduː ə 'krɒswɜːd/
jog (v)	/dʒɒg/
play golf (v)	/ˌpleɪ 'gɒlf/
read a book (v)	/ˌriːd ə 'bʊk/
sunbathe (v)	/'sʌnbeɪð/
swim (v)	/swɪm/
at the moment	/ˌæt ðə 'məʊmənt/
deliver (v)	/dɪ'lɪvə(r)/
get wet (v)	/ˌget 'wet/
give someone a lift (v)	/ˌgɪv sʌmwʌn ə 'lɪft/
heavy (adj)	/'hevi/
nowhere (adv)	/'nəʊweə(r)/
stand (v)	/stænd/
wake up (v)	/ˌweɪk 'ʌp/

19
transport sign (n)	/'trænspɔːt ˌsaɪn/
crossroads (n pl)	/'krɒsrəʊdz/
dead end (n)	/ˌded 'end/
no entry	/ˌnəʊ 'entri/
roadworks (n pl)	/'rəʊdwɜːks/
sharp bend (n)	/ˌʃɑːp 'bend/
steep hill (n)	/ˌstiːp 'hɪl/

20
give someone a hand (with ...)? (exp)	/ˌgɪv ˌsʌmwʌn ə 'hænd wɪθ/
It's OK. (exp)	/ɪts ˌəʊ'keɪ/
Sure (exp).	/ʃɔː/
That's very kind. (exp)	/ˌðæts ˌveri 'kaɪnd/
by the way (exp)	/ˌbaɪ ðə 'weɪ/
just a minute (exp)	/ˌdʒʌst ə 'mɪnɪt/
show someone around (v)	/ˌʃəʊ sʌmwʌn ə'raʊnd/

21
along the street (exp)	/əˌlɒŋ ðə 'striːt/
at the bottom of the hill (exp)	/æt ðə ˌbɒtəm əv ðə 'hɪl/
at the end of the road (exp)	/æt ði ˌend əv ðə 'rəʊd/
at the top of the hill (exp)	/æt ðə ˌtɒp əv ðə 'hɪl/
down the hill (exp)	/ˌdaʊn ðə 'hɪl/
in the middle of the square (exp)	/ɪn ðə ˌmɪdl əv ðə 'skweə/
into the car park (exp)	/ˌɪntə ðə 'kɑː ˌpɑːk/
on the corner of the street (exp)	/ɒn ðə ˌkɔːnə(r) əv ðə 'striːt/
out of the car park (exp)	/ˌaʊt əv ðə 'kɑː ˌpɑːk/
over the bridge (exp)	/ˌəʊvə(r) ðə 'brɪdʒ/
past the shop (exp)	/ˌpɑːst ðə 'ʃɒp/
round the park (exp)	/ˌraʊnd ðə 'pɑːk/
turn left (exp)	/ˌtɜːn 'left/
turn right (exp)	/ˌtɜːn 'raɪt/
through the park (exp)	/ˌθruː ðə 'pɑːk/
under the bridge (exp)	/ˌʌndə(r) ðə 'brɪdʒ/
up the hill (exp)	/ˌʌp ðə 'hɪl/

22
cash machine (n)	/'kæʃ məˌʃiːn/
Excuse me. (exp)	/ɪk'skjuːz mi/
shop window (n)	/ˌʃɒp 'wɪndəʊ/
sweatshirt (n)	/'swetʃɜːt/
wait for (v)	/'weɪt fɔː/
while (conj)	/waɪl/

23
corridor (n)	/'kɒrɪdɔː/
dig (v)	/dɪg/
have a rest (v)	/ˌhæv ə 'rest/
impossible (adj)	/ɪm'pɒsəbl/
knock (v)	/nɒk/
point to (v)	/'pɔɪnt tu/
restaurant (n)	/'restrɒnt/
stay at (v)	/'steɪ ˌæt/
waiter (n)	/'weɪtə(r)/

24
junction (n)	/'dʒʌŋkʃn/
roundabout (n)	/'raʊndəbaʊt/
traffic lights (n pl)	/'træfɪk laɪts/
shopping centre (n)	/'ʃɒpɪŋ ˌsentə(r)/
on the left-hand side (exp)	/ɒn ðə ˌleft hænd 'saɪd/
on the right-hand side (exp)	/ɒn ðə ˌraɪt hænd 'saɪd/
After about ... (exp)	/'ɑːftə(r) əbaʊt/
how to get there (exp)	/haʊ tə 'get ˌðeə/
Go along ... (v) (exp)	/ˌgəʊ ə'lɒŋ/
Look for ... (v) (exp)	/lʊk fɔː(r)/
Take the second turning on the left. (exp)	/teɪk ðə 'sekənd ˌtɜːnɪŋ ɒn ðə 'left/
go straight on (exp)	/ˌgəʊ streɪt 'ɒn/
speed limit	/'spiːd ˌlɪmɪt/
Interstate Highway (n)	/'ɪntəsteɪt ˌhaɪweɪ/
mile (n)	/maɪl/
motorway (n)	/'məʊtəweɪ/

Review 25–32

Vocabulary

1 Name six places. Use the words.

~~sea~~ desert ocean islands lake river

The Mediterranean Sea

2 Look at the pictures. Complete the text with the correct words.

Mary Jones is in her ¹*twenties / sixties*. She is ²*short / tall* and fairly ³*slim / overweight*. She has ⁴*medium-length / short* dark hair. Her brother James is ⁵*young / middle-aged*. He is very ⁶*short / tall*. He has very ⁷*dark / fair* hair. He's got a ⁸*moustache / beard*.

Grammar

3 Make sentences with the correct form of *going to*.

1 Manos _is going to meet_ his girlfriend. (meet)
2 _____ Hajer and Naila _____ dinner? (make)
3 I _____ TV tonight. (not / watch)
4 _____ you _____ your sister? (phone)
5 _____ Rosanna _____ tomorrow? (study)
6 The match _____ at three o'clock. (start)
7 We _____ to the party. (not / go)

4 Write the adverbs.

1 easy *easily*
2 good
3 bad
4 quick
5 fast
6 careful

5 Tick ✓ or correct the sentences.

1 He doesn't sing very ~~good~~. *well*
2 The meal was excellent.
3 They play badly football.
4 India sounds beautifully.
5 She's a terribly teacher.
6 This is an easily exercise.
7 The wine tastes awful.

Skills

6 Read the text and answer the questions.

Last week John bought an old boat. He's going to repair it and paint it red. In June he's going to leave England and sail to Greece. It's going to take two months to get to Greece. On the way, he's going to visit France, Spain, Morocco, and Italy. He isn't going to go alone. His wife is going to stay in England, but John's going to take his cat, Errol.

1 What did John buy last week?
2 Who is going to repair and paint the boat?
3 When is John going to arrive in Greece?
4 How many countries is John going to visit?
5 Is John's wife going to go with him?
6 Who is Errol?

7 Match the sentences with the responses.

1 Do you like swimming? __
2 Which shirt do you like? __
3 I love shopping. __
4 Sara doesn't like cooking. __

a I prefer the blue one.   c No, I hate it.
b Really? I don't mind it.   d Do you? I can't stand it.

8 Write the opposites.

1 selfish
2 hard-working
3 quiet
4 confident

English for Everyday Life

9 Complete the conversations.

know   maybe   sure   probably

1 A Is Milo going to quit his job?
  B Yes, _____.
2 A Are you going to go to the party?
  B _____.
3 A When does your course start?
  B We don't _____ yet.
4 A Where is Emily?
  B I'm not _____.

10 Put the words in the correct order to make shopping expressions.

1 Can I help you?

1 help I Can you ?
2 this pen How is much ?
3 I take 'll it .
4 you see Would the one other like to ?
5 that Can have I one ?

Wordlist 25–32

25 Africa (n) /'æfrɪkə/
Antarctica (n) /æn'tɑːktɪkə/
Asia (n) /'eɪʒə/
Europe (n) /'jʊərəp/
Lake Victoria (n) /ˌleɪk vɪk'tɔːriə/
Mount Everest (n) /ˌmaʊnt 'evərɪst/
North America (n) /ˌnɔːθ ə'merɪkə/
Oceania (n) /ˌəʊʃi'ɑːniə/
South America (n) /ˌsaʊθ ə'merɪkə/
The Amazon (n) /ði 'æməzən/
The Arctic Ocean (n) /ði ˌɑːktɪk 'əʊʃn/
The Atlantic Ocean (n) /ði ətˌlæntɪk 'əʊʃn/
The Canary Islands (n) /ðə kə'neəri ˌaɪləndz/
The Indian Ocean (n) /ðə ˌɪndiən 'əʊʃn/
The Mediterranean Sea (n) /ðə ˌmedɪtə'reɪniən 'siː/
The Pacific Ocean (n) /ðə pəˌsɪfɪk 'əʊʃn/
The Rockies (n) /ðə 'rɒkiz/
The Sahara Desert (n) /ðə səˌhɑːrə 'dezət/
The South Pole (n) /ðə ˌsaʊθ 'pəʊl/

26 advert (n) /'ædvɜːt/
exactly (adv) /ɪg'zæktli/
have an early night (v) /hæv ˌən 'ɜːli 'naɪt/
I can't believe it. (exp) /aɪ ˌkɑːnt bɪ'liːv ɪt/
robot (n) /'rəʊbɒt/
the news (n) /ðə 'njuːz/

27 east (n) /iːst/
north (n) /nɔːθ/
south (n) /saʊθ/
west (n) /west/
all over /ɔːl 'əʊvə(r)/
boat (n) /bəʊt/
break a record (v) /ˌbreɪk ə 'rekɔːd/
continent (n) /'kɒntɪnənt/
European (adj) /ˌjʊərə'piːən/
marathon (n) /'mærəθən/
race (n) /reɪs/
rally (n) /ræli/
River Thames (n) /ˌrɪvə(r) 'temz/
speedboat (n) /'spiːdbəʊt/
take (v) /teɪk/
take part in (v) /teɪk 'pɑːt ɪn/
unusual (adj) /ʌn'juːʒuəl/
vintage car (n) /ˌvɪntɪdʒ 'kɑː(r)/
Wales (n) /weɪlz/
yacht (n) /jɒt/

28 Maybe. (exp) /'meɪbi/
We aren't sure. (exp) /wi ˌɑːnt 'ʃɔː/
We don't know yet. (exp) /wi ˌdəʊnt 'nəʊ, 'jet/
Yes, probably. (exp) /ˌjes 'prɒbəbli/

29 build (n) /bɪld/
medium build (adj) /ˌmiːdiəm 'bɪld/
medium height (adj) /ˌmiːdiəm 'haɪt/
overweight (adj) /ˌəʊvə'weɪt/
short (adj) /ʃɔːt/
slim (adj) /slɪm/
tall (adj) /tɔːl/
general appearance (n) /ˌdʒenrəl ə'pɪərəns/
attractive (adj) /ə'træktɪv/
good-looking (adj) /ˌgʊd'lʊkɪŋ/
handsome (adj) /'hænsəm/
pretty (adj) /'prɪti/
age (n) /eɪdʒ/
in his/her seventies (exp) /ˌɪn hɪz /hə 'sevntiz/
middle-aged (adj) /ˌmɪdl 'eɪdʒd/
young (adj) /jʌŋ/
hair (n) /heə(r)/
bald (adj) /bɔːld/
beard (n) /bɪəd/
blonde (adj) /blɒnd/
brown (adj) /braʊn/
curly (adj) /'kɜːli/
dark (adj) /dɑːk/
fair (adj) /feə(r)/
medium length (adj) /ˌmiːdiəm 'leŋθ/
moustache (n) /mə'stɑːʃ/
long (adj) /lɒŋ/
straight (adj) /streɪt/
wavy (adj) /'weɪvi/

30 badly (adv) /'bædli/
delicious (adj) /dɪ'lɪʃəs/
excellent (adj) /'eksələnt/
perfect (adj) /'pɜːfekt/
perfectly (adv) /'pɜːfektli/
terrible (adj) /'terəbl/
well (adj) /wel/

31 I can't stand ... (exp) /aɪ ˌkɑːnt' stænd/
I don't mind ... (exp) /aɪ ˌdəʊnt 'maɪnd/
confident (adj) /'kɒnfɪd(ə)nt/
generous (adj) /'dʒenərəs/
hard-working (adj) /ˌhɑːd'wɜːkɪŋ/
lazy (adj) /'leɪzi/
quiet (adj) /'kwaɪət/
noisy (adj) /'nɔɪzi/
selfish (adj) /'selfɪʃ/
shy (adj) /ʃaɪ/

32 have a look at (v) /ˌhæv a 'lʊk ət/
Can I help you? (exp) /kən aɪ 'help juː/
How much are those ... ? (exp) /haʊ mʌtʃ ə 'ðəʊz/
I think I prefer ... (exp) /aɪ 'θɪŋk aɪ prɪ'fɜː(r)/
I'll take it. (exp) /aɪl 'teɪk ɪt/

Vocabulary

1 Write six kinds of TV programme.

a documentary,

2 Complete the conversations.

headache	sick	painful	~~temperature~~
burnt	flu	rash	bleeding

1 **A** What's her <u>temperature</u>?
   B It's quite high, 39ºC.
2 **A** My back itches.
   B Yes, you've got a _____ .
3 **A** My finger's _____ .
   B Don't worry. I've got some plasters.
4 **A** What's the matter?
   B I feel _____ .
5 **A** I've got a _____ .
   B Here, I've got some painkillers.
6 **A** I've got _____ .
   B Oh, dear. Stay in bed then.
7 **A** My knee is swollen.
   B Is it very _____ ?
8 **A** I've _____ my finger.
   B Put it under some cold water.

Grammar

3 Make questions and sentences with the present perfect. Use the cues.

1 Have you ever been to Tunisia?

1 you / ever / go / to Tunisia?
2 He / never / fail / an exam.
3 they / ever / visit / Madrid?
4 We / never / win / anything.
5 she / ever / be / on TV?

4 Choose the correct form.

1 **A** What's Sam's phone number?
   B Er, I've *forgotten / forgot*.
2 **A** When *have you seen / did you see* Toni?
   B Last Saturday.
3 **A** Can you play golf on Tuesday?
   B No, sorry. I've *broken / broke* my thumb.
4 **A** Where's Hannah?
   B She's *gone / went* to a meeting.
5 **A** Oh, no! We've *missed / missed* the bus.
   B There's another one in five minutes.
6 **A** Is Fred here?
   B No. He's *gone / went* at 3.30.

Skills

5 Choose the correct words.

1 Thieves have stolen €100 million from Best Bank. The money *is / isn't* in the bank now.
2 The new Olympic stadium has opened. You *can / can't* use the stadium now.
3 The US president has arrived in Beijing. The president is in *Beijing / the US* now.
4 A fire has destroyed ten houses in Birmingham. People *can / can't* live in the houses now.

6 Complete the advice to travellers.

water	legs and feet	hand luggage
comfortable	toiletry items	~~vaccinations~~

1 See your doctor for your <u>vaccinations</u> .
2 Don't forget to pack your _____, such as toothpaste and a hairbrush.
3 Drink lots of _____ to avoid dehydration.
4 When you are sitting down, move your _____ .
5 Wear _____ clothes.
6 Put your money in your _____ .

English for Everyday Life

7 Match the halves of the expressions.

1 What seems to __   a hurt?
2 When did __   b at your chest?
3 Can I have a look __   c check it.
4 Where does it __   d be the problem?
5 We'd better __   e the pain start?

33
TV programme (n)	/ˌtiː ˈviː ˌprəʊɡræm/
cartoon (n)	/kɑːˈtuːn/
chat show (n)	/ˈtʃæt ˌʃəʊ/
documentary (n)	/ˌdɒkjuˈmentri/
film (n)	/fɪlm/
game show (n)	/ˈɡeɪm ˌʃəʊ/
hospital drama (n)	/ˈhɒspɪtl ˌdrɑːmə/
movie (n)	/ˈmuːvi/
music programme (n)	/ˈmjuːzɪk ˌprəʊɡræm/
police drama (n)	/pəˈliːs ˌdrɑːmə/
reality TV show (n)	/riˌæləti tiː ˈviː ˌʃəʊ/
sitcom (n)	/ˈsɪtkɒm/
soap opera (n)	/ˈsəʊp ˌɒprə/
sports programme (n)	/ˈspɔːts ˌprəʊɡræm/
the news (n)	/ðə ˈnjuːz/
TV advert (n)	/ˌtiː ˈviː ˌædvɜːt/
weather forecast (n)	/ˈweðə(r) ˌfɔːkɑːst/
channel (n)	/ˈtʃænl/
commercial (adj)	/kəˈmɜːʃl/
licence fee (n)	/ˈlaɪsns ˌfiː/
newsreader (n)	/ˈnjuːz ˌriːdə(r)/
satellite TV (n)	/ˌsætəlaɪt ˌtiː ˈviː/
subscription (n)	/səbˈskrɪpʃn/

34
lottery (n)	/ˈlɒtəri/
lucky (adj)	/ˈlʌki/
millions of pounds (exp)	/ˌmɪljənz əv ˈpaʊndz/
miss a plane (v)	/ˌmɪs ə ˈpleɪn/
prize (n)	/praɪz/
ride a horse (v)	/ˌraɪd ə ˈhɔːs/
save someone's life (v)	/ˌseɪv sʌmwʌnz ˈlaɪf/
ticket	/ˈtɪkɪt/
unlucky (adj)	/ʌnˈlʌki/
wow (exp)	/waʊ/
win (v)	/wɪn/

35
accident (n)	/ˈæksɪd(ə)nt/
award (n)	/əˈwɔːd/
coast (n)	/kəʊst/
crash into (v)	/ˌkræʃ ˈɪntu/
destroy (v)	/dɪˈstrɔɪ/
diamond (n)	/ˈdaɪəmənd/
head of government (n)	/ˌhed əv ˈɡʌvənmənt/
headline (n)	/ˈhedlaɪn/
hit (v)	/hɪt/
kill (v)	/kɪl/
latest (adj)	/ˈleɪtɪst/
prime minister (n)	/ˌpraɪm ˈmɪnɪstə(r)/
thief (n)	/θiːf/
tropical storm (n)	/ˌtrɒpɪkl ˈstɔːm/

36
I believe ... (exp)	/aɪ bɪˈliːv/
I think ... (exp)	/aɪ ˈθɪŋk/
No, I don't think so. (exp)	/ˈnəʊ aɪ dəʊnt ˈθɪŋk səʊ/
Yes, I think so. (exp)	/ˈjes aɪ ˈθɪŋk səʊ/

37
health problem (n)	/ˈhelθ ˌprɒbləm/
I've bruised my leg. (exp)	/aɪv ˌbruːzd maɪ ˈleɡ/
I've burnt my hand. (exp)	/aɪv ˌbɜːnt maɪ ˈhænd/
I've cut my finger. (exp)	/aɪv ˌkʌt maɪ ˈfɪŋɡə(r)/
I feel sick. (exp)	/aɪ fiːl ˈsɪk/
I've got a cold. (exp)	/aɪv ˌɡɒt ə ˈkəʊld/
I've got a rash. (exp)	/aɪv ˌɡɒt ə ˈræʃ/
I've got a temperature. (exp)	/aɪv ˌɡɒt ə ˈtemprɪˌtʃə/
I've got an infection. (exp)	/aɪv ˌɡɒt ən ɪnˈfekʃn/
I've got flu. (exp)	/aɪv ɡɒt ˈfluː/
I've hurt my knee. (exp)	/aɪv ˌhɜːt maɪ ˈniː/
I've sprained my ankle. (exp)	/aɪv ˌspreɪnd maɪ ˈæŋkl/
My arm itches. (exp)	/maɪ ˈɑːm ɪtʃɪz/
My thumb's painful. (exp)	/maɪ ˈθʌmz ˌpeɪnfl/
My nose is bleeding. (exp)	/maɪ ˈnəʊz ɪz ˌbliːdɪŋ/
My elbow's swollen. (exp)	/maɪ ˈelbəʊz ˌswəʊlən/

38
bone (n)	/bəʊn/
break (v)	/breɪk/
downstairs (adv)	/ˌdaʊnˈsteəz/
drop (v)	/drɒp/
fall (v)	/fɔːl/
fall off (v)	/fɔːl ˈɒf/
happen (v)	/ˈhæpən/
hurt (v)	/hɜːt/

39
avoid (v)	/əˈvɔɪd/
charger (n)	/ˈtʃɑːdʒə(r)/
dehydration (n)	/ˌdiːhaɪˈdreɪʃn/
hairbrush (n)	/ˈheəbrʌʃ/
insect bite (n)	/ˈɪnsekt ˌbaɪt/
jewellery (n)	/ˈdʒuːəlri/
knife (n)	/naɪf/
luggage (n)	/ˈlʌɡɪdʒ/
medical item (n)	/ˈmedɪkl ˌaɪtəm/
medicine (n)	/ˈmedsn/
mobile phone (n)	/ˌməʊbaɪl ˈfəʊn/
painkiller (n)	/ˈpeɪnkɪlə(r)/
plaster (n)	/ˈplɑːstə(r)/
scissors (n pl)	/ˈsɪzəz/
suitcase (n)	/ˈsuːtkeɪs/
sunscreen (n)	/ˈsʌnskriːn/
tablet (n)	/ˈtæblət/
toiletry item (n)	/ˈtɔɪlətri ˌaɪtəm/
toothbrush (n)	/ˈtuːθbrʌʃ/
toothpaste (n)	/ˈtuːθpeɪst/
vaccination (n)	/ˌvæksɪˈneɪʃn/
valid (adj)	/ˈvælɪd/

40
have a look at (v)	/hæv ə ˈlʊk æt/
In the meantime ... (exp)	/ɪn ðə ˈmiːntaɪm/
We'd better check your ... (exp)	/wiːd ˈbetə(r) tʃek jɔː(r)/
What seems to be the problem? (exp)	/wɒt ˌsiːmz tə biː ðə ˈprɒbləm/

Review 41–48

Vocabulary

1 Choose the correct word.

1 peel *potatoes* / ~~chips~~
2 roast *a chicken* / *an omelette*
3 *grill* / *boil* an egg
4 *pour* / *slice* water
5 put food on a *bowl* / *plate*
6 a *mixed* / *stirred* salad

2a Match the items with the shops.

1 chicken *c*
2 painkillers ___
3 onions ___
4 magazines ___
5 paper and pens ___

a a stationery shop
b a newsagent's
c a butcher's
d a chemist's
e a greengrocer's

b Write four more shops. Say one thing you can buy in each shop.

Grammar

3 Complete the recipe.

a	~~slices~~	grams	four	little
some	many	few	an	much

For Scrambled Eggs on Toast you need:
two [1] *slices* of bread, [2] ___ large eggs, 100
[3] ___ of butter.
Toast the bread and put it on [4] ___ plate.
Mix the eggs in a bowl with a [5] ___ milk. Add
[6] ___ salt. Put the butter in a saucepan and pour
the eggs and milk into the pan. Cook the eggs for a
[7] ___ minutes. Serve on the toast.
This is [8] ___ easy recipe, it doesn't take [9] ___
time and you don't need [10] ___ things.

4 Write the comparative and superlative forms.

nice	big	noisy	popular	good	bad

nicer, the nicest

5 Complete the sentences. Use the comparative or superlative form of the adjective in brackets.

1 Spain is _smaller than_ China. (small)
2 My car is ___ car in the world. (slow)
3 Maths is ___ Geography. (bad)
4 This is ___ room in the house. (big)
5 Her laptop was ___ Tom's. (cheap)
6 Reading was ___ thing in Chinese. (difficult)
7 Heidi is ___ Hans. (friendly)
8 The Riviera is ___ restaurant in town. (expensive)

Skills

6 Read the text. Are the statements true (T) or false (F)?

Last year Sally heard about the Tomato Soup Diet. Every day you have four bowls of soup and three litres of water. It sounded boring but it was a fast way to lose weight. On the first day she bought some tomatoes at the market and made lots of soup. It was delicious, and she lost three kilos in five days. On the sixth day she felt sick and she didn't have much energy so she decided to stop the diet and have a big plate of steak and chips.

1 The soup was made of meat.
2 She bought the soup at the market.
3 She liked the soup.
4 She lost three kilos on the diet.
5 She was on the diet for seven days.
6 She had lots of energy.

7 Answer the questions.

1 What shops are there near your house?
2 Do you go to a market? What do you buy there?
3 Where do you do most of your food shopping? Why?

English for Everyday Life

8 Complete the expressions.

serious	believe	not	for

1 Oh, ___ goodness sake!
2 You can't be ___!
3 Oh no, ___ again!
4 Oh, I don't ___ it!

9 Match the questions with the responses.

1 Is that any good? *c*
2 What size is that? ___
3 Can I try this on, please? ___
4 It's too tight. ___
5 Anything else? ___

a Yes, the changing rooms are over there.
b No, thanks.
c Yes. This one's fine.
d Extra large.
e This one is a bigger size.

Wordlist 41–48

41
bowl (n)	/bəʊl/
frying pan (n)	/ˈfraɪɪŋ ˌpæn/
plate (n)	/pleɪt/
saucepan (n)	/ˈsɔːspən/
bake (v)	/beɪk/
boil (v)	/bɔɪl/
fry (v)	/fraɪ/
grill (v)	/ɡrɪl/
roast (v)	/rəʊst/
add (v)	/æd/
mix (v)	/mɪks/
peel (v)	/piːl/
pour (v)	/pɔː(r)/
slice (v)	/slaɪs/
stir (v)	/stɜː(r)/
weigh (v)	/weɪ/

42
fruit (n)	/fruːt/
milk (n)	/mɪlk/
raspberry (n)	/ˈrɑːzbəri/
strawberry (n)	/ˈstrɔːbəri/
sugar (n)	/ˈʃʊɡə(r)/
water (n)	/ˈwɔːtə(r)/
wine (n)	/waɪn/
fork (n)	/fɔːk/
knife (n)	/naɪf/
spoon (n)	/spuːn/
any (det)	/ˈeni/
bottle (n)	/ˈbɒtl/
a few (det)	/ə ˈfjuː/
gram (n)	/ɡræm/
kilo (n)	/ˈkiːləʊ/
a little (det)	/ə ˈlɪtl/
many (det)	/ˈmeni/
much (det)	/mʌtʃ/
piece (n)	/piːs/
slice (n)	/slaɪs/
some (det)	/sʌm/

43
but	/bʌt/
however	/haʊˈevə(r)/
a couple (n)	/ə ˈkʌpl/
lots (n)	/lɒts/
basic rule (n)	/ˌbeɪsɪk ˈruːl/
diet (n)	/ˈdaɪət/
energy (n)	/ˈenədʒi/
full (adj)	/fʊl/
lose weight (v)	/ˌluːz ˈweɪt/
read about (v)	/ˈriːd əˌbaʊt/

44
Oh no, not again! (exp)	/əʊ ˌnəʊ nɒt əˈgen/
Oh, for goodness sake! (exp)	/əʊ fə ˌɡʊdnəs ˈseɪk/
Oh, I don't believe it! (exp)	/əʊ aɪ ˌdəʊnt bɪˈliːv ɪt/
You can't be serious! (exp)	/juː ˌkaːnt bi ˈsɪəriəs/
You must be joking! (exp)	/juː ˌmʌst bi ˈdʒəʊkɪŋ/

45
baker's (n)	/ˈbeɪkəz/
butcher's (n)	/ˈbʊtʃəz/
chemist's (n)	/ˈkemɪsts/
department store (n)	/dɪˈpaːtmənt ˌstɔː(r)/
estate agent's (n)	/ɪˈsteɪt ˌeɪdʒənts/
flower shop (n)	/ˈflaʊə ˌʃɒp/
furniture shop (n)	/ˈfɜːnɪtʃə ˌʃɒp/
greengrocer's (n)	/ˈɡriːnɡrəʊsəz/
hairdresser's (n)	/ˈheədresəz/
hardware shop (n)	/ˈhaːdweə ˌʃɒp/
jewellery shop (n)	/ˈdʒuːəlri ˌʃɒp/
music shop (n)	/ˈmjuːzɪk ˌʃɒp/
newsagent's (n)	/ˈnjuːzeɪdʒənts/
sports shop (n)	/ˈspɔːts ˌʃɒp/
stationery shop (n)	/ˈsteɪʃnri ˌʃɒp/
travel agent's (n)	/ˈtrævl ˌeɪdʒənts/

46
best (adj)	/best/
better (adj)	/ˈbetə(r)/
busy (adj)	/ˈbɪzi/
far (adj)	/ˈfaː(r)/
friendly (adj)	/ˈfrendli/
popular (adj)	/ˈpɒpjələ(r)/
safe (adj)	/ˈseɪf/
tidy (adj)	/ˈtaɪdi/
worse	/wɜːs/
worst	/wɜːst/

47
convenient (adj)	/kənˈviːniənt/
fresher (adj)	/ˈfreʃə(r)/
home delivery (n)	/ˌhəʊm dɪˈlɪvəri/
on the other hand (exp)	/ɒn ði ˈʌðə(r) hænd/
personal (adj)	/ˈpɜːsənl/
shopping centre (n)	/ˈʃɒpɪŋ ˌsentə(r)/
street market (n)	/ˈstriːt ˌmaːkɪt/

48
changing room (exp)	/ˈtʃeɪndʒɪŋ ˌruːm/
How is it? (exp)	/haʊ ˈɪz ɪt/
Is that any good? (exp)	/ɪz ˌðæt eni ˈɡʊd/
size (n)	/saɪz/
try on (v)	/traɪ ˈɒn/
Buy now pay later (exp)	/baɪ ˌnaʊ peɪ ˈleɪtə(r)/
Buy one get one free (exp)	/ˈbaɪ wʌn ˌget wʌn ˈfriː/
Closing down sale (n)	/ˌkləʊzɪŋ daʊn ˈseɪl/
Everything must go (exp)	/ˌevriθɪŋ mʌst ˈgəʊ/
sale 50 % off	/seɪl ˈfɪfti pəˌsent ˈɒf/
special offer (n)	/ˌspeʃl ˈɒfə(r)/
Two for the price of one (exp)	/ˌtuː fə ðə praɪs əv ˈwʌn/
enough (adv)	/ɪˈnʌf/
extra large (adj)	/ˌekstrə ˈlaːdʒ/
loose (adj)	/luːs/
medium (adj)	/ˈmiːdiəm/
tight (adj)	/taɪt/
too (adv)	/tuː/

Review 49–56

Vocabulary

1 Put the words in the correct column.

~~spend~~	PIN number	coins	pay
borrow	foreign currency	cheque	lend
notes	bank account		

Verbs	Bank	Cash
spend		

2 Complete the sentences. Use verbs from exercise 1.

1 How much money do you _____ on clothes?
2 Do you want me to _____ you some money?
3 Can I _____ €10? I haven't got any money.
4 We usually _____ by cheque.

3 Match the sentence halves.

1 I'd like to try water _d_   a diving?
2 Davide loves collecting __   b DIY.
3 I don't mind doing __   c the Internet?
4 They haven't tried mountain __   d skiing.
5 Do you like surfing __   e climbing.
6 Has she tried scuba __   f things.

Grammar

4 Complete the text. Use the verbs in brackets.

In five years' time I ¹*'ll be__* (be) rich. I ²_____ (not / live) in Ireland. I ³_____ (move) to Brazil. I ⁴_____ (buy) a house and I ⁵_____ (learn) Portuguese, but I ⁶_____ (not / find) a job. I ⁷_____ (relax) all day and I ⁸_____ (go) clubbing at night. I ⁹_____ (not / be) married and I ¹⁰_____ (not / have) any children.

5 Make sentences about your life in five years' time.

1 What kind of job will you have? *I'll be a doctor.*
2 Where will you be?
3 Will you have a house or an apartment?
4 Will you be married or single?
5 How many children will you have?

6 Make sentences with the first conditional. Use the cues.

1 *You won't get wet if you take an umbrella.*
1 You / not / get wet / if / you / take / an umbrella.
2 He / buy / a car / if / he / pass / his driving test.
3 If / they / leave / now / they / not / miss / the train.
4 If / the weather / be / horrible / we / not / go out.
5 I / get / some coffee / if / I / go out.
6 If / I / see Jan / I / tell / him / about the meeting.

Skills

7 Read the text. Choose the correct answers.

If you like food, you'll love this holiday in Vietnam. You'll start in Hanoi and spend three nights at the Hotel Annam. We'll take you to the market, where you'll learn how to choose the best food, then our chef will show you how to prepare typical Vietnamese food. After that, you'll leave the north of Vietnam and fly south to Ho Chi Minh City. You'll have four days there and learn to cook 'bo bay mon', a seven-part beef dinner. When you aren't in the kitchen, there will be visits to some of Vietnam's ancient temples and monuments.

1 The main activity is ~~shopping~~ / cooking.
2 The Hotel Annam is in Hanoi / Ho Chi Minh City.
3 You'll visit two / three places.
4 Ho Chi Minh City is in the north / south of Vietnam.
5 'Bo bay mon' is a kind of food / monument.
6 You can sunbathe / go sightseeing.

English for Everyday Life

8 Put the words in the correct order to make expressions.

1 *It's losing money.*
1 losing 's money It .
2 isn't good Business very .
3 bad a It price isn't .
4 can't We it afford .
5 will How that cost much ?

9 Put the sentences in the correct order to make a conversation.

a _2_ How many nights is that for?
b __ And how many guests will there be?
c _1_ I'd like to make a reservation for 11 May, please.
d __ Four nights.
e __ Fine. The price will be €100.
f __ Does that include breakfast?
g __ One – me. And I'd like a sea view, please.
h __ Yes, it does.

Wordlist 49–56

49 bank (n) — /bæŋk/
bank account (n)) — /ˈbæŋk əˌkaʊnt/
cheque (n) — /tʃek/
credit card (n) — /ˈkredɪt ˌkɑːd/
PIN number (n) — /ˈpɪn ˌnʌmbə(r)/
salary (n) — /ˈsæləri/
cash (n) — /kæʃ/
change (n) — /tʃeɪndʒ/
coin (n) — /kɔɪn/
foreign currency (n) — /ˌfɒrən ˈkʌrənsi/
note (n) — /nəʊt/
receipt (n) — /rɪˈsiːt/
borrow (v) — /ˈbɒrəʊ/
exchange (v) — /ɪksˈtʃeɪndʒ/
lend (v) — /lend/
pay (n) — /peɪ/
save (v) — /seɪv/
spend (v) — /spend/
abroad (adj) — /əˈbrɔːd/
electronically (adv) — /ɪˌlekˈtrɒnɪkli/
enter (v) — /ˈentə(r)/
cash machine (n) — /ˈkæʃ məˌʃiːn/
insert (v) — /ɪnˈsɜːt/
remove (v) — /rɪˈmuːv/

50 computer chip (n) — /kəmˈpjuːtə(r) ˌtʃɪp/
email (v) — /ˈiːmeɪl/
future (n) — /ˈfjuːtʃə(r)/
prediction (n) — /prɪˈdɪkʃn/
text (n) — /tekst/
work from home (v) — /ˌwɜːk frəm ˈhəʊm/

51 actually (adv) — /ˈæktʃuəli/
appear (v) — /əˈpɪə(r)/
book a holiday (v) — /ˌbʊk ə ˈhɒlədeɪ/
diesel (n) — /ˈdiːzl/
disease (n) — /dɪˈziːz/
electricity (n) — /ɪˌlekˈtrɪsəti'/
global warming (n) — /ˌgləʊbl ˈwɔːmɪŋ/
hydrogen (n) — /ˈhaɪdrədʒən/
keyboard (n) — /ˈkiːbɔːd/
population (n) — /ˌpɒpjuˈleɪʃn/
powerful (adj) — /ˈpaʊəfl/
space (n) — /speɪs/
transport (n) — /ˈtrænspɔːt/
war (n) — /wɔː(r)/

52 afford (v) — /əˈfɔːd/
broke (adj) — /brəʊk/
Business isn't very good. (exp) — /ˈbɪznəs ɪznt veri ˌgʊd/
cost (v) — /kɒst/
lose money (exp) — /ˌluːz ˈmʌni/
not a bad price (exp) — /ˌnɒt ə bæd ˈpraɪs/

53 canoeing — /kəˈnuːɪŋ/
clubbing — /ˈklʌbɪŋ/
collecting things — /kəˈlektɪŋ ˌθɪŋz/
doing DIY — /ˌduːɪŋ diː aɪ ˈwaɪ/
going out with — /ˌgəʊɪŋ ˈaʊt wɪð/
going to the gym — /ˌgəʊɪŋ tə ðə ˈdʒɪm/
mountain-climbing — /ˈmaʊntən ˌklaɪmɪŋ/
painting — /ˈpeɪntɪŋ/
relaxing — /rɪˈlæksɪŋ/
sailing — /ˈseɪlɪŋ/
scuba-diving — /ˈskuːbə ˌdaɪvɪŋ/
sightseeing — /ˈsaɪtsiːɪŋ/
surfing the Internet — /ˌsɜːfɪŋ ði ˈɪntənet/
sunbathing — /ˈsʌnbeɪðɪŋ/
water-skiing — /ˈwɔːtəskiɪŋ/

54 autumn (n) — /ˈɔːtəm/
spring (n) — /sprɪŋ/
winter (n) — /ˈwɪntə(r)/
cherry blossom (n) — /ˈtʃeri ˌblɒsəm/
crowded (n) — /ˈkraʊdɪd/
Japan (n) — /dʒəˈpæn/
lunch break (n) — /ˈlʌntʃ breɪk/
postcard (n) — /ˈpəʊstkɑːd/
stay in (v) — /steɪ ˈɪn/
visa (n) — /ˈviːzə/

55 ancient monument (n) — /ˌeɪnʃənt ˈmɒnjumənt/
by the sea (exp) — /ˌbaɪ ðə ˈsiː/
coral reef (n) — /ˌkɒrəl ˈriːf/
explore (v) — /ɪkˈsplɔː(r)/
extra (adj) — /ˈekstrə/
five-star (adj) — /faɪv stɑː(r)/
have a massage (v) — /ˌhæv ə ˈmæsɑːʒ/
holiday guide (n) — /ˈhɒlədeɪ gaɪd/
rainforest (n) — /ˈreɪnfɒrɪst/
resort (n) — /rɪˈzɔːt/
swimming pool (n) — /ˈswɪmɪŋ puːl/
tropical fish (n) — /ˌtrɒpɪkl ˈfɪʃ/
yacht (n) — /jɒt/

56 Does that include … ? (exp) — /dʌz, ðæt ɪnˈkluːd/
How many … ? (exp) — /haʊ ˈmeni/
I'd like to … (exp) — /aɪd ˈlaɪk tu/
We'd like … (exp) — /wiːd ˈlaɪk/
What name is it? (exp) — /ˌwɒt ˈneɪm ɪz ɪt/
When for? (exp) — /ˌwen ˈfɔː(r)/
bed and breakfast (n) — /bed ən ˈbrekfəst/
Do not disturb. (exp) — /ˌduː nɒt dɪˈstɜːb/
lobby (n) — /ˈlɒbi/
reception (n) — /rɪˈsepʃn/
vacancies (n pl) — /ˈveɪkənsiz/

Review 57–64

Vocabulary

1a Look at the definitions. Write the missing letters.

1 You sit on this.
a _chair_

2 You put rubbish in this.
a w_ _ _ _ _ b_ _

3 You make copies with this.
a p _ _ _ _ _ _ _ _ _ _

4 You put books on this.
a s_ _ _ _ _

5 You keep files in this.
a f_ _ _ _ _ _ c_ _ _ _ _ _ _

b Write four more office items.

a computer

2a Match the halves of the words.

1 a washing _e_   a cleaner
2 an air __   b radio
3 an electric __   c conditioner
4 a light __   d player
5 a vacuum __   e machine
6 a DVD __   f fan
7 a clock __   g bulb

b What things do you use in your home?

I use a washing machine,

Grammar

3 Julia is a secretary. Look at the table. Make six sentences about her job. Use _has to / must_, _doesn't have to_, or _mustn't_.

She must arrive on time.

Necessary	Not necessary	Not allowed
arrive on time	make coffee for the boss	wear jeans
answer the phone	do shift work	smoke in the office

4 Rewrite the advice. Use _should / shouldn't_.

1 _You shouldn't drink alcohol and drive._

1 Don't drink alcohol and drive.
2 Have a holiday.
3 Go to the doctor's.
4 Don't eat lots of chocolate.
5 Get a new car.
6 Don't stand on the table.

Skills

5 Read the text. Answer the questions.

In Scotland about 13,000 people a year die because they smoke cigarettes. In 2004 the Scottish Parliament passed a new law. Since 2006, people can't smoke in public places (pubs, cafés, restaurants, offices). In a pub in Glasgow we asked people about the new law.

Jimmy Kenzie: Well, I work in this pub. I don't smoke so I think the new law is a good idea.

Rod Dunbar: I agree with Jimmy. The pub is much nicer now and we can smoke in the pub garden.

Mary Brown: In my opinion the law is a bad idea. Now I have to smoke outside in the rain.

1 How many people in Scotland die each year because they smoke?
2 What public places does the writer mention?
3 When was the new law passed?
4 Where are the people?
5 Who thinks the law is a good idea?
6 Who thinks the law is a bad idea?
7 Has your country got a law like this?

English for Everyday Life

6 Complete the greetings.

let	surprise	take	nice	~~come~~

1 Hi, Petra. _Come_ on in.
2 _____ a seat.
3 _____ me get you a drink.
4 This is a nice _____.
5 It's _____ to see you.

7 Read the dialogues. Complete the words.

1 **A** Why is there water in the kitchen?
B The washing machine is l_ea_k_i_ng.

2 **A** Can I borrow your camera?
B I'm sorry, it isn't w _ _ _ ing.

3 **A** Are you going to buy that kettle?
B No, it's sc_ _ t_ h_ d.

4 **A** Why aren't you wearing your new shirt?
B It's t_ _ n.

5 **A** What's wrong with this jumper?
B It's got a big h_ _ e in it.

Wordlist 57–64

57
cupboard (n)	/ˈkʌbəd/
filing cabinet (n)	/ˈfaɪlɪŋ ˌkæbɪnət/
photocopier (n)	/ˈfəʊtəʊkɒpiə(r)/
printer (n)	/ˈprɪntə(r)/
shelf (n)	/ʃelf/
waste bin (n)	/ˈweɪst bɪn/
do some filing (v)	/ˌduː səm ˈfaɪlɪŋ/
do some photocopying (v)	/ˌduː səm ˈfəʊtəʊkɒpiɪŋ/
go on the Internet (v)	/ˌgəʊ ɒn ði ˈɪntənet/
go to a meeting (v)	/ˌgəʊ tu ə ˈmiːtɪŋ/
have a break (v)	/ˌhæv ə ˈbreɪk/
have a day off (v)	/ˌhæv ə deɪ ˈɒf/
make a phone call (v)	/ˌmeɪk ə ˈfəʊn ˌkɔːl/
make an appointment (v)	/ˌmeɪk ən əˈpɔɪntmənt/
send an email (v)	/ˌsend ən ˈiːmeɪl/
send a letter (v)	/ˌsend ə ˈletə(r)/

58
don't have to (modal)	/dəʊnt ˈhæv tu/
have to (modal)	/ˈhæv tu/
must (modal)	/mʌst/
mustn't (modal)	/ˈmʌsnt/

59
a couple of hours (exp)	/ə ˌkʌpl əv ˈaʊəz/
an hour (exp)	/ən ˈaʊə(r)/
an hour and a half (exp)	/ən ˌaʊə(r) ənd ə ˈhɑːf/
an hour and a quarter	/ən ˌaʊə(r) ənd ə ˈkwɔːtə(r)/
half an hour (exp)	/ˌhɑːf ən ˈaʊə(r)/
two and a half hours (exp)	/ˌtuː ənd ə hɑːf ˈaʊə(r)z/
by car (adv)	/baɪ ˈkɑː(r)/
come home (v)	/ˌkʌm ˈhəʊm/
journey (n)	/ˈdʒɜːni/
rush hour (n)	/ˈrʌʃ aʊə(r)/
school run (n)	/ˈskuːl rʌn/
summer (n)	/ˈsʌmə(r)/
take (time) (v)	/teɪk/
take the train (v)	/ˌteɪk ðə ˈtreɪn/
traffic jam (n)	/ˈtræfɪk dʒæm/

60
Come on in. (exp)	/ˌkʌm ɒn ˈɪn/
surprise	/səˈpraɪz/
Take a seat. (exp)	/ˌteɪk ə ˈsiːt/
accept (v)	/əkˈsept/
hard (adj)	/hɑːd/
have a look (v)	/hæv ə ˈlʊk/
I don't believe it! (exp)	/aɪ ˌdəʊnt bɪˈliːv ɪt/
refuse (v)	/rɪˈfjuːz/
subject (n)	/ˈsʌbdʒɪkt/

61
air conditioner (n)	/ˈeə(r) kəndɪʃənə(r)/
clock radio (n)	/ˌklɒk ˈreɪdiəʊ/
dishwasher (n)	/ˈdɪʃwɒʃə(r)/
DVD player (n)	/ˌdiː viː ˈdiː ˌpleɪə(r)/
electric fan (n)	/ɪˌlektrɪk ˈfæn/
hairdryer (n)	/ˈheədraɪə(r)/
heater (n)	/ˈhiːtə(r)/
kettle (n)	/ˈketl/
light bulb (n)	/ˈlaɪt bʌlb/
microwave (n)	/ˈmaɪkrəweɪv/
shaver (n)	/ˈʃeɪvə(r)/
toaster (n)	/ˈtəʊstə(r)/
vacuum cleaner (n)	/ˈvækjuəm ˌkliːnə(r)/
washing machine (n)	/ˈwɒʃɪŋ məˌʃiːn/
clean the car (v)	/ˌkliːn ðə ˈkɑː(r)/
clean the windows (v)	/ˌkliːn ðə ˈwɪndəʊz/
cook the dinner (v)	/ˌkʊk ðə ˈdɪnə(r)/
do the shopping (v)	/ˌduː ðə ˈʃɒpɪŋ/
do the ironing (v)	/ˌduː ði ˈaɪənɪŋ/
do the washing up (v)	/ˌduː ðə wɒʃɪŋ ˈʌp/
lay the table (v)	/ˌleɪ ðə ˈteɪbl/
make breakfast (v)	/ˌmeɪk ˈbrekfəst/
make the beds (v)	/ˌmeɪk ðə ˈbedz/
take out the rubbish (v)	/ˌteɪk aʊt ðə ˈrʌbɪʃ/
tidy the garden (v)	/ˌtaɪdi ðə ˈgɑːdn/
tidy the room (v)	/ˌtaɪdi ðə ˈruːm/

62
should (modal)	/ʃʊd/
shouldn't (modal)	/ˈʃʊdnt/
caution (n)	/ˈkɔːʃn/
floor (n)	/flɔː(r)/
Mind your head. (exp)	/ˌmaɪnd yɔː ˈhed/
slippery (exp)	/ˈslɪpəri/
touch (exp)	/tʌtʃ/
warning (n)	/ˈwɔːnɪŋ/

63
agree (v)	/əˈgriː/
I don't think so. (exp)	/aɪ ˌdəʊnt ˈθɪŋk səʊ/
In my opinion, ... (exp)	/ɪn ˈmaɪ əpɪnjən/
good idea (n)	/ˌgʊd aɪˈdɪə/
domestic job (n)	/dəˈmestɪk dʒɒb/
housework (n)	/ˈhaʊswɜːk/
introduce a law (v)	/ɪntrəˌdjuːs ə ˈlɔː/
pass a law (v)	/ˌpɑːs ə lɔː/
share (v)	/ʃeə(r)/

64
It isn't working. (exp)	/ɪt ˌɪznt ˈwɜːkɪŋ/
It's damaged. (exp)	/ɪts ˈdæmɪdʒd/
It's got a hole in it. (exp)	/ɪts gɒt ə ˈhəʊl ɪn ɪt/
It's leaking. (exp)	/ɪts ˈliːkɪŋ/
It's scratched. (exp)	/ɪts skrætʃt/
It's torn. (exp)	/ɪts tɔːn/
exchange (n)	/ɪksˈtʃeɪndʒ/
receipt (n)	/rɪˈsiːt/
refund (n)	/ˈriːfʌnd/

Vocabulary

1a Look around you. Write six things that you can see.

a cupboard

b What is each thing made of?

The cupboard is made of wood.

c Write four more materials.

2 Match the computer words with the definitions.

1 click *b*
2 restart ___
3 quit ___
4 shut down ___
5 a folder ___
6 the desktop ___

a turn off your computer
b press on a button on the mouse
c you see icons and windows on this
d you save your files here
e finish using a program
f turn your computer off then on again

Grammar

3 Make sentences with the present simple passive. Use the cues.

1 Newspapers and magazines are saved.

1 Newspapers and magazines / save.
2 Green bins / deliver to people's houses.
3 Newspapers / put into the bins.
4 The paper / collect.
5 It / take to the recycling centre.
6 The paper / clean.
7 It / use to make newspapers.

4 Complete the sentences. Use the past simple passive of the words in brackets.

1 Millions of plastic bottles *were sold* (sell) last year.
2 Only 3% of the bottles _____ (recycle).
3 Some of the plastic _____ (use) to make clothes.
4 A lot of money _____ (save).
5 More recycling centres _____ (open).

5 Choose the correct relative pronoun.

1 That's the man *who / which* repaired my car.
2 She's the actress *that / which* was in *Titanic*.
3 These are the books *who / that* we borrowed.
4 This is the CD player *who / which* isn't working.
5 People *that / which* are rich aren't always happy.
6 Are these the jeans *who / that* you bought?

Skills

6 Read the text. Are the statements true (T) or false (F)?

Bonfire Night

In 1605 a man named Guy Fawkes tried to destroy the Houses of Parliament in London. His plan failed and he was caught. Every year, on 5 November, people in England celebrate this. Big models of Guy Fawkes are made from newspaper and old clothes. People build big fires in their gardens and the guy is put on top and burnt. There are lots of parties and people eat baked potatoes and a special 'bonfire' cake.

1 Guy Fawkes tried to destroy London.
2 Guy Fawkes' plan didn't fail.
3 Bonfire Night is celebrated every year.
4 Models of the Houses of Parliament are made from newspaper.
5 The guy is burnt outdoors.
6 People bake bread and eat fruit.

7 Read Cecilia's details. Complete her profile.

Name: Cecilia
Age: 33
From: Cartagena (north-west Colombia).
Job: secretary
Appearance: quite tall, slim, brown eyes, brown hair
Hobbies: reading, the theatre
Likes: friendly people
Looking for: someone to go to the theatre with

My name's ¹*Cecilia* . I'm ²_____ years old and I'm from ³_____ in ⁴_____ . I'm a ⁵_____ in a factory. I'm ⁶_____ and slim. I've got ⁷_____ and brown hair. My hobbies are reading and ⁸_____ . I like people who are ⁹_____ . I'm looking for someone who wants to ¹⁰_____ .

English for Everyday Life

8 Put the words in the correct order to make expressions.

1 Oh, know I that didn't .
2 sure you Are ?
3 you Yes, 're right .
4 's true That .

Wordlist 65–72

65
cardboard (n)	/ˈkɑːdbɔːd/
cotton (n)	/ˈkɒtn/
glass (n)	/glɑːs/
gold (n)	/gəʊld/
leather (n)	/ˈleðə(r)/
metal (n)	/ˈmetl/
paper (n)	/ˈpeɪpə(r)/
plastic (n)	/ˈplæstɪk/
rubber (n)	/ˈrʌbə(r)/
silver (n)	/ˈsɪlvə(r)/
wood (n)	/wʊd/
wool (n)	/wʊl/
It's made of … (exp)	/ɪts ˈmeɪd əv/
recycle (v)	/ˌriːˈsaɪkl/

66
build (v)	/bɪld/
by hand (adv)	/baɪ ˈhænd/
check (v)	/tʃek/
colleague (n)	/ˈkɒliːg/
destroy (v)	/dɪˈstrɔɪ/
explosion (n)	/ɪkˈspləʊʒn/
history programme (n)	/ˈhɪstri ˌprəʊgræm/
hobby (n)	/ˈhɒbi/
model (n)	/ˈmɒdl/
normal (adj)	/ˈnɔːml/
plan (n)	/plæn/
plant (n)	/plɑːnt/
produce (v)	/prəˈdjuːs/
real (adj)	/ˈriːəl/
second (n)	/ˈsekənd/
(a) sixth (n)	/sɪksθ/

67
greetings card (n)	/ˈgriːtɪŋz ˌkɑːd/
anniversary (n)	/ænɪˈvɜːsəri/
birth (n)	/bɜːθ/
Christmas (n)	/ˈkrɪsməs/
death (n)	/deθ/
Father's Day (n)	/ˈfɑːðə(r)z ˌdeɪ/
Mother's Day (n)	/ˈmʌðə(r)z ˌdeɪ/
Valentine's Day (n)	/ˈvæləntaɪnz ˌdeɪ/
celebrate (v)	/ˈselɪbreɪt/
dead (n)	/ded/
festival (n)	/ˈfestɪvl/
rainy season (n)	/ˈreɪni ˌsiːzn/
relative (n)	/ˈrelətɪv/

68
Are you sure? (exp)	/ˌɑː juː ˈʃɔː(r)/
That's true. (exp)	/ˈðæts truː/
right (adj)	/raɪt/
block (n)	/blɒk/
meanwhile (adv)	/ˈmiːnwaɪl/
sign (v)	/saɪn/
tell (v)	/tel/
work (v)	/wɜːk/

69
attachment (n)	/əˈtætʃmənt/
cursor (n)	/ˈkɜːsə(r)/
desktop (n)	/ˈdesktɒp/
file (n)	/faɪl/
folder (n)	/ˈfəʊldə(r)/
icon (n)	/ˈaɪkɒn/
menu (n)	/ˈmenjuː/
menu bar (n)	/ˈmenjuː ˌbɑː(r)/
program (n)	/ˈprəʊgræm/
window (n)	/ˈwɪndəʊ/
click (v)	/klɪk/
close (v)	/kləʊz/
delete (v)	/dɪˈliːt/
open (v)	/ˈəʊpən/
quit (v)	/kwɪt/
re-start (v)	/ˌriːˈstɑːt/
save (v)	/seɪv/
scroll down (v)	/ˌskrəʊl ˈdaʊn/
shut down (v)	/ˌʃʌt ˈdaʊn/

70
that (pron)	/ðæt/
which (pron)	/wɪtʃ/
who (pron)	/huː/

71
active (adj)	/ˈæktɪv/
businessman (n)	/ˈbɪznəsmæn/
city professional (n)	/ˌsɪti prəˈfeʃnl/
drunk (adj)	/drʌŋk/
ex-partner (n)	/ˌeks ˈpɑːtnə(r)/
honest (adj)	/ˈɒnɪst/
interest (n)	/ˈɪntrəst/
Internet dating (n)	/ˌɪntənet ˈdeɪtɪŋ/
last (v)	/lɑːst/
love life (n)	/ˈlʌv laɪf/
online (adj)	/ˌɒnˈlaɪn/
ordinary-looking (adj)	/ˈɔːdnri ˌlʊkɪŋ/
outdoor activity (n)	/ˌaʊtdɔː(r) ækˈtɪvəti/
profile (n)	/ˈprəʊfaɪl/
psychologist (n)	/saɪˈkɒlədʒɪst/
sporty (adj)	/ˈspɔːti/
suburbs (n pl)	/ˈsʌbɜːbz/

72
adaptor (n)	/əˈdæptə(r)/
architect (n)	/ˈɑːkɪtekt/
carry (v)	/ˈkæri/
civil engineer (n)	/ˌsɪvl endʒɪˈnɪə(r)/
electrical appliance (n)	/ɪˌlektrɪkl əˈplaɪəns/
football pitch (n)	/ˈfʊtbɔːl pɪtʃ/
plug (n)	/plʌg/
relation (n)	/rɪˈleɪʃn/
screen (n)	/skriːn/
screensaver (n)	/ˈskriːnseɪvə(r)/
stadium (n)	/ˈsteɪdiəm/
pipe (n)	/paɪp/

Vocabulary

1 Complete the phrasal verbs.

away	up	~~back~~	on	for	down

1 Oh, you're busy. I'll come _back_ later.
2 Put _____ a jumper, or you'll be cold.
3 The photocopier has broken _____.
4 What are you looking _____?
5 Turn _____ the TV. We can't hear it.
6 Don't throw _____ that letter. I need it.

2a Choose the correct word.

1 My job is *boring / bored* and my boss is always *miserable / proud*. She was *annoying / annoyed* this morning because I was late.
2 Benji was *exciting / excited* about going scuba-diving for the first time, but he was also a little *worrying / worried*. However, it was really *interesting / interested*.

b How do you feel now? Why?

Grammar

3 Put the time expressions in the correct column.

~~ages~~	a few years	~~last Monday~~	July
1987	a long time	two months	three o'clock

for	since
ages	last Monday

4 Complete the sentences. Use the present perfect or the past simple.

1 I'm divorced. I _____ married for six years. (be)
2 We _____ here for a long time and we like it. (live)
3 He _____ the piano since he was 12. (play)
4 I _____ here since one o'clock. (be)
5 She's retired. She _____ in a shop for 40 years. (work)

5 Make questions and sentences with the second conditional. Use the cues.

1 *Would you help him if he asked you?*

1 you / help / him / if / he / ask / you?
2 She / do / more exercise / if / she / have / more time.
3 If / I / lose / my job / I / find / another.
4 If / Yanni / find / some money / he / not / spend it.
5 We / save / our dog / if / our house / be / on fire.
6 you / marry me / if / I / win the lottery?

Skills

6a Read the text. Answer the questions.

Mark	
	I still live in Leeds and am happily married with three children.

Kerry	
	I live in Bristol with my husband and our daughter, Jane. I'm a doctor. We left Leeds in 1992.

Emily	
	Divorced, living in Leeds, two sons. I'd love to hear from old friends.

Jim	
	Accountant in New York. Left England and spent five years teaching in Chile. Single.

1 Which people have moved to another place?
   Kerry, Jim.
2 How many people have got children?
3 Who isn't married?
4 Which countries has Jim lived in?
5 Who has changed his / her job?

b Write an entry for a school website for yourself.

English for Everyday Life

7 Complete the note.

just	~~dear~~	presents	delicious
thank you	wishes	hope	really

¹ *Dear* Miriam

We're ² _____ writing to say ³ _____ for the Christmas ⁴ _____ that you sent. The chocolates were ⁵ _____ and we ⁶ _____ like the fruit bowl.

⁷ _____ to see you soon.

Best ⁸ _____

Julia and Phil

73
break down (v)	/ˌbreɪk 'daʊn/
come back (v)	/ˌkʌm 'bæk/
come in (v)	/ˌkʌm 'ɪn/
get up (v)	/ˌget 'ʌp/
go away (v)	/ˌgəʊ ə'weɪ/
go out (v)	/ˌgəʊ 'aʊt/
look after (v)	/ˌlʊk 'ɑːftə(r)/
look back (v)	/ˌlʊk 'bæk/
look down (v)	/ˌlʊk 'daʊn/
look for (v)	/'lʊk fɔː(r)/
look up (v)	/ˌlʊk 'ʌp/
put on (v)	/ˌpʊt 'ɒn/
switch off (v)	/ˌswɪtʃ 'ɒf/
switch on (v)	/ˌswɪtʃ 'ɒn/
take off (v)	/ˌteɪk 'ɒf/
throw away (v)	/ˌθrəʊ ə'weɪ/
try on (v)	/ˌtraɪ 'ɒn/
turn down (v)	/ˌtɜːn 'daʊn/
turn up (v)	/ˌtɜːn 'ʌp/

74
away (adv)	/ə'weɪ/
each other (pron)	/iːtʃ 'ʌðə(r)/
for (prep)	/fɔː(r)/
boring (adj)	/'bɔːrɪŋ/
lovely (adj)	/'lʌvli/
meat (n)	/miːt/
nearly (adv)	/'nɪəli/
since (prep)	/sɪns/
vegetarian (n)	/ˌvedʒə'teəriən/

75
How are you? (exp)	/ˌhaʊ ə 'juː/
It's good to see you. (exp)	/ɪts gʊd tə 'siː ju/
event (n)	/ɪ'vent/
former (adj)	/'fɔːmə(r)/
free time (n)	/ˌfriː 'taɪm/
insurance company (n)	/ɪn'ʃʊərəns ˌkʌmpəni/
raise money (v)	/ˌreɪz 'mʌni/
reunion (n)	/riː'juːniən/
same (adj)	/seɪm/

76
answer the phone (v)	/'ɑːnsə ðə ˌfəʊn/
hang up (v)	/ˌhæŋ 'ʌp/
I'll try his mobile. (exp)	/aɪl ˌtraɪ hɪz 'məʊbaɪl/
no reply (exp)	/ˌnəʊ rɪ'plaɪ/
re-charge (v)	/ˌriː'tʃɑːdʒ/
ring (v)	/rɪŋ/
empty (adj)	/'empti/
on the way (exp)	/ˌɒn ðə 'weɪ/
solicitor (n)	/sə'lɪsɪtə(r)/

77
annoyed (adj)	/ə'nɔɪd/
annoying (adj)	/ə'nɔɪɪŋ/
bored (adj)	/bɔːd/
confused (adj)	/kən'fjuːzd/
confusing (adj)	/kən'fjuːzɪŋ/
embarrassed (adj)	/ɪm'bærəst/
embarrassing (adj)	/ɪm'bærəsɪŋ/
excited (adj)	/ɪk'saɪtɪd/
exciting (adj)	/ɪk'saɪtɪŋ/
frightened (adj)	/'fraɪtnd/
frightening (adj)	/'fraɪtnɪŋ/
hungry (adj)	/'hʌngri/
interested (adj)	/'ɪntrəstɪd/
miserable (adj)	/'mɪzrəbl/
proud (adj)	/praʊd/
relaxed (adj)	/rɪ'lækst/
surprised (adj)	/sə'praɪzd/
thirsty (adj)	/'θɜːsti/
tired (adj)	/'taɪəd/
tiring (adj)	/'taɪərɪŋ/
worried (adj)	/'wʌrid/

78
certificate (n)	/sə'tɪfɪkət/
document (n)	/'dɒkjumənt/
get out (v)	/ˌget 'aʊt/
on fire	/ˌɒn 'faɪə/
pet (n)	/pet/
replace (v)	/rɪ'pleɪs/
valuable (adj)	/'væljuəbl/
wallet (n)	/'wɒlɪt/
would (modal)	/wʊd/

79
after a while (exp)	/ˌæftə(r) ə 'waɪl/
again and again (exp)	/ə'gen ənd ə.gen/
at first (exp)	/æt 'fɜːst/
for a long time (exp)	/fɔː(r) ə ˌlɒŋ 'taɪm/
for a (short) while (exp)	/fɔː(r) ə ˌʃɔːt 'waɪl/
in the end (exp)	/ˌɪn ði 'end/
material things (n pl)	/mə'tɪəriəl θɪŋz/
memory (n)	/'meməri/
psychology (n)	/saɪ'kɒlədʒi/
skydiving (n)	/'skaɪdaɪvɪŋ/

80 & Epilogue
All the best (exp)	/ˌɔːl ðə 'best/
Best wishes (exp)	/ˌbest 'wɪʃɪz/
Hope to see you soon. (exp)	/ˌhəʊp tu ˌsiː ju 'suːn/
I hope you're well .(exp)	/aɪ ˌhəʊp jɔː 'wel/
I'm just writing to say ... (exp)	/aɪm dʒʌst ˌraɪtɪŋ tə seɪ/
Just a note to say ... (exp)	/dʒʌst ə ˌnəʊt tə seɪ/
Love (exp)	/lʌv/
Thank you for ... (exp)	/'θæŋk ju fɔː(r)/
calm down (exp)	/ˌkɑːm 'daʊn/
stupid (adj)	/'stjuːpɪd/

Grammar reference

Lessons 1–4

to be

Statements					
Positive			**Negative**		
I	'm		I	'm not	
He She It	's (is)	married.	He She It	isn't (is not)	Italian.
We You They	're (are)		We You They	aren't (are not)	

Questions

To make questions with *to be* we put the verb in front of the subject.

1 *yes / no* questions and short answers
   Statement: **He is** from Korea.

   Question: **Is he** from Korea?   Yes, he is.
   No, he isn't.

   Statement: **They are** married.

   Question: **Are they** married?   Yes, they are.
   No, they aren't.

2 *wh-* questions
   Where **are you** from?
   When **is your birthday**?

have / has got

We use *have / has got* to talk about:
   possessions   I've got a car.
   family   Have you got any brothers and sisters?
   descriptions   He's got short hair.

Positive and negative statements			
I You We They	've (have) haven't (have not)	got	a mobile phone. two brothers. dark hair.
He She It	's (has) hasn't (has not)		

Questions

To make questions with *have got*, we put *have / has* in front of the subject.

1 *yes / no* questions and short answers
   Statement: **He has** got a brother.

   Question: **Has he** got a brother?   Yes, he has.
   No, he hasn't.

   Statement: **You have** got my address.

   Question: **Have you** got my address?   Yes, I have.
   No, I haven't

2 *wh-* questions
   How many children **have you** got?
   What kind of car **has she** got?

Lessons 5–8

Present simple

We use the present simple for:
1 **permanent states**
   I **like** chocolate.
   They **live** in Hong Kong.

2 **regular activities**
   We **get up** at six o'clock.
   She **plays** tennis on Saturdays.

Positive statements		
I You We They	live work	in France.
He She It	lives works	

Spelling		
Verbs ending in -ss, -sh, -ch or -o, add -es.	miss finish watch go	misses finishes watches goes
When the verb ends in -y, we change the -y to -ies.	study	studies

Grammar reference

Negative statements

I You We They	don't (do not)	live work	here.
He She It	doesn't (does not)		

yes / no questions

Do	I you we they	live work	in India?
Does	he she it		

NOTE In negatives and questions we use the infinitive form of the verb.
She doesn't **live** here.
NOT ~~She doesn't lives here.~~
Does he **play** rugby?
NOT ~~Does he plays rugby?~~

Short answers

Positive			Negative		
Yes,	I you we they	do.	No,	I you we they	don't. (do not)
	he she it	does.		he she it	doesn't. (does not)

wh- questions
Where **do you** live?
When **does he** go to work?

Adverbs of frequency

1 Adverbs of frequency show how often something happens.

0% -- 100%
never   rarely   sometimes   often   usually   always
                                             normally

2 We put the adverb of frequency:
– after the verb *to be*   She's **always** here at 4.30.
– in front of a normal verb   We **often** eat at this café.
– between an auxiliary   They don't **usually** work
   and the main verb   on Sundays.

Prepositions of time

1 We use *in* with:

years	in 2003
months	in September
seasons	in winter
parts of the day	in the afternoon
BUT	at night

2 We use *on* with:

days	on Tuesday
dates	on 9 August
parts of a specific day	on Monday morning

3 We use *at* with:

times	at seven o'clock
the weekend	at the weekend

Lessons 9–12

Past simple: positive and negative statements

We use the past simple to talk about completed events in the past.

to be

I He She It	was wasn't (was not)	at work on holiday away	last week. yesterday.
We You They	were weren't (were not)		

Grammar reference

Regular verbs

NOTE The past simple is the same for all subjects.

For most verbs, we add -ed.	play	played
	watch	watched
When the verb ends in -e, we add -d.	close	closed
	like	liked
When the verb ends in a short vowel and a single consonant, we double the consonant and add -ed.	drop	dropped
	grab	grabbed
When the verb ends in -y, we change the -y to -ied.	hurry	hurried

NOTE When the verb ends in -t or -d, we pronounce the final syllable /ɪd/:
wanted /wɒntɪd/
needed /niːdɪd/

Irregular verbs

Many common verbs have an irregular past form.

go   They **went** skiing last month.
see   I **saw** that film yesterday.

See the list of irregular verbs on page 123.

Negative statements

I He She It We You They	didn't (did not)	cook the meal. go shopping. have lunch.

NOTE After *didn't* we use the infinitive form of the verb.

We didn't **like** the play.
NOT ~~We didn't liked the play.~~

He didn't **go** to work.
NOT ~~He didn't went to work.~~

because and *so*

1 **We use *because* to give a reason or cause.**
   I didn't go to work, **because** I was ill.

2 **We use *so* to show a result or effect.**
   I was ill, **so** I didn't go to work.

Lessons 13–16

Years

We normally give years like this:
   1853   eighteen fifty-three   2042   twenty forty-two
   1902   nineteen oh two

NOTE For 2000 to 2009 we say *two thousand (and) ...*
   2004   two thousand and four

Past simple: questions and short answers

The verb *to be*
To make questions with *to be* we put the verb in front of the subject.

1 *yes / no* questions and short answers
   Statement: **She was** on holiday.

   Question: **Was she** on holiday?   Yes, she was.
                                            No, she wasn't.

   Statement: **They were** at home.

   Question: **Were they** at home?   Yes, they were.
                                           No, they weren't.

2 *wh-* questions
   Where **were you** last week?
   When **was the party**?

Regular and irregular verbs

yes / no questions		
Did	I he she it we you they	like the film? go skiing? pay the bill?

Short answers					
Positive			**Negative**		
Yes,	I he she it we you they	did.	No,	I he she it we you they	didn't.

Grammar reference

3 *wh-* questions

What **did you** do?

When **did they** leave?

NOTE In questions we use the infinitive form of the verb.

Did you **stay** in a hotel?

NOT ~~Did you stayed in a hotel?~~

What did you **buy**?

NOT ~~What did you bought?~~

Infinitive of purpose

We use an infinitive to show why somebody does something.

We went to the shops.

Why did you go?

We went to the shops **to buy** a new computer.

Lessons 17–20

Present continuous

1 We use the present continuous to say what is happening at the moment.

They're **playing** football at the moment.

I'm **wearing** jeans today.

2 We make the present continuous with the verb *to be* and the *-ing* form of the verb (the present participle).

Statements

Positive			Negative		
I	'm (am)		I	'm not (am) not	
He She It	's (is)	swimming. eating.	He She It	isn't (is not)	jogging. listening.
We You They	're (are)		We You They	aren't (are not)	

Spelling

1 For verbs that end in *-e*, we remove the *-e* and add *-ing*.

write   writing

use   using

2 For verbs with a short vowel and only one consonant, we double the consonant and add *-ing*.

run   running

stop   stopping

Questions

To make questions we put the verb *to be* in front of the subject.

1 *yes / no* questions and short answers

Statement: **He is** waiting for the bus.

Question: **Is he** waiting for the bus?   Yes, he is.
                                                No, he isn't.

Statement: **They are** having a break.

Question: **Are they** having a break?   Yes, they are.
                                               No, they aren't.

2 *wh-* questions

Where **are you** going?

What **is she** wearing?

Present simple and present continuous

1 We use the present simple for regular activities.

They **play** tennis on Saturdays.

We often use these expressions with the present simple:

often, always, every day, usually, on Tuesdays

2 We use the present continuous to say what is happening at the moment.

They **aren't playing** tennis today, because it**'s raining**.

They**'re watching** TV at the moment.

We often use these expressions with the present continuous:

now, at the moment, today, this morning

Stative verbs

We don't normally use these verbs in the present continuous form even when they refer to the present moment:

like, love, prefer, hate, want, need

I **want** to listen to the radio.

NOT ~~I'm wanting to listen to the radio.~~

Grammar reference

Lessons 21–24

Past continuous

1 We use the past continuous for an activity in progress in the past.
I **was waiting** for the bus.
The men **were having** a break.

2 We make the past continuous with the past simple of the verb *to be* and the *-ing* form of the verb (the present participle).

Positive and negative statements

I He She It	was wasn't (was not)	going to the bank. having a shower. wearing jeans.
We You They	were weren't were not	

Questions

To make questions we put *was* or *were* in front of the subject.

1 *yes/no* questions and short answers
Statement: **He was** wearing a jacket.

Question: **Was he** wearing a jacket?   Yes, he was.
                                        No, he wasn't.

Statement: **You were** having dinner.

Question: **Were you** having dinner?   Yes, we were
                                        No, we weren't.

2 *wh-* questions
Where **were they** standing?
What **was she** doing?

Past continuous and past simple

1 The past continuous describes an event in progress in the past.
I **was having** a bath.

2 The past simple shows a completed action or event in the past.
The doorbell **rang**.

3 We often use the past continuous and the past simple together. The past continuous sets the scene.

The past simple says what happened. We usually join the clauses with *while*, *as*, or *when*.
While I **was having** a bath, the doorbell **rang**.

I was having a bath.
- →
                    ↑
        The doorbell rang.

4 We use two past simple verbs when two things happened, one after the other.

When the doorbell **rang**, I **got out** of the bath.

- →
            ↑   ↑
The doorbell rang.   I got out of the bath.

Lessons 25–28

Articles with geographical names

The	
rivers	The Amazon
seas	The Black Sea
oceans	The Atlantic (Ocean)
deserts	The Kalahari (Desert)
mountain ranges	The Alps
groups of islands	The Bahamas
some countries	The USA, The UK, The Czech Republic

No *The*	
mountains	Mount Fuji
lakes	Lake Balaton
continents	Africa
countries	Morocco
islands	Sicily

going to

We use *going to* for:

1 intentions and decisions
We**'re going to** have a party.

2 a definite future
Look at those clouds. It**'s going to** rain.

Grammar reference

Positive and negative statements

I	'm (am) 'm not (am not)		
He She It	's (is) isn't (is not)	going to	have a sandwich. go windsurfing. watch a DVD. play the piano.
We You They	're (are) aren't (are not)		

Questions

To make questions with *going to*, we put the verb *am*, *is*, or *are* in front of the subject.

1 *yes / no* questions and short answers

Statement: **She is** going to buy a car.

Question: **Is she** going to buy a car?   Yes, she is.
No, she isn't.

Statement: **You are** going to leave.

Question: **Are you** going to leave?   Yes, I am.
No, I'm not.

2 *wh-* questions
How **are you** going to travel?
What **are you** going to do?

Large numbers

1 **We separate large numbers with a comma.**
25,000   twenty-five thousand
6,000,000   six million

2 **We say:**
twenty-five **thousand** kilometres.
NOT ~~twenty-five thousands kilometres.~~
six **million** people
NOT ~~six millions of people~~

Lessons 29–32

Adjectives and adverbs

1 **An adjective describes a noun.**
He's a **slow** driver.
This is an **easy** exercise.
2 **An adverb describes a verb.**
He drives **slowly**.
You can do this exercise **easily**.

	Adjective	Adverb
+ *ly*	slow bad careful	slowly badly carefully
- *y* + *ily*	easy busy	easily busily
- *le* + *ly*	terrible horrible	terribly horribly
Irregular	good fast	well fast

like + -ing

To talk about likes and dislikes with activities we usually use the *-ing* form of the verb.
Do you like **meeting** new people?
We hate **jogging**.
I prefer **skating** to **skiing**.
For the spelling rules of the *-ing* forms, see Lessons 17–20 above.

one / ones

We normally use *one* or *ones* as a pronoun after an adjective.
Do you like this coat?
I prefer the black **one**. (i.e. the black coat)

Can I have a look at those bags, please?
The big **ones** or the small **ones**? (i.e. the big bags or the small bags)

Grammar reference

Lessons 33–36

Present perfect

1 We use the present perfect to talk about experiences in our life up to the present.
I**'ve ridden** a camel.
Have you ever **done** yoga?
We often use *ever* and *never* with the present perfect.
Have you **ever** been to Brazil?
I've **never** flown in a helicopter.

Positive and negative statements

I You We They	've (have) haven't (have not)	seen the Pyramids. slept in a tent.
He She It	's (has) hasn't (has not)	worked abroad. been to Russia.

2 We make the present perfect with the verb *have / has* and the past participle of the verb.
To form regular past participles, we add *-ed* to the verb stem.
play   played
live   lived

This is the same as the regular past. (See Lessons 9–12 above for spelling rules.)

3 Verbs with an irregular past simple also have an irregular past participle.

Infinitive	Past simple	Past participle
do	did	done
see	saw	seen
take	took	taken

See the list of irregular verbs on page 123.

Questions

To make questions with the present perfect, we put *have / has* in front of the subject.

1 *yes / no* questions and short answers
Statement: **He has** worked abroad.

Question: **Has he** worked abroad?   Yes, he has.
No, he hasn't.

Statement: **You have** eaten sushi.

Question: **Have you** eaten sushi?   Yes, I have.
No, I haven't

2 *wh-* questions
How many times **have you** been to Australia?
What sports **have you** played?

been and *gone*

1 In the present perfect we use *been* instead of *gone* when we are talking about our experiences.
Have you ever **been** to Indonesia?
Yes, I have.

I've never **been** hang-gliding.

2 *Been* means *go and come back*.
I've **been** to Berlin.   I'm not in Berlin now.
He's **gone** to Berlin.   He's in Berlin now.

Present perfect with present result

We use the present perfect for a past action with a result in the present. We don't know when the action happened, and it isn't important.
They**'ve gone** to China.   They're in China now.
A storm **has destroyed**   You can't use the bridge
the bridge.   now.
She**'s lost** her keys.   She can't find her keys now.

Lessons 37–40

Possessive adjectives

We use a possessive adjective when we talk about a part of the body.
Her leg's swollen.
I've hurt **my** hand.
You've got a bruise on **your** leg.

Present perfect and past simple

1 The present perfect links the past with the present.

Now.

We use it for:
– a past action with a result in the present.
She**'s gone out**.   She isn't at home now.
We**'ve had** lunch.   We aren't hungry now.

– experiences up to the present.

I**'ve been** to New York three times. (up to now)

He**'s** never **broken** his arm. (up to now)

2 The past simple describes a completed action in the past.

Now

We use it when:

– we are interested in the action itself not the effect.

I've hurt my leg. I **fell off** a ladder.

– when we are interested in the actual time of the event.

I **saw** John yesterday.

NOTE When there is a past time reference (*yesterday, last year, in November*), we must use the past simple, not the present perfect.

I **saw** John yesterday.

NOT ~~I've seen John yesterday.~~

Lessons 41–44

Expressing quantity

1 Some nouns are countable. They have a singular and a plural form.

You need an **apple**.   You need some **apples**.

2 Some nouns are uncountable. They have only one form.

You need some **fruit**.

3 These things are usually uncountable:

– **Drinks** coffee, tea, wine, water, beer, milk
– **Food** which you only eat part of bread, cheese, fish meat
– **Things** which you only use part of toothpaste, shampoo, soap
– **Materials** paper, wood, plastic
– **Some general words** music, money, information

4 We use these articles and quantity expressions with countable and uncountable nouns:

Countable nouns

Singular	a/an	You need **a** knife.
		He's got **an** apple.
Plural	some/any	You need **some** strawberries.
		We haven't got **any** strawberries.
		Have you got **any** apples?
	How many	**How many** apples do you need?
	not many	We don't need **many** apples.
	a few	We need **a few** blackcurrants.

Uncountable nouns

One form	some/any	You need **some** bread.
		We haven't got **any** milk.
		Have you got **any** fruit?
	How much	**How much** bread do you need?
	not much	We don't need **much** bread.
	a little	We need **a little** milk.

5 To talk about quantities of an uncountable noun we use quantity expressions, e.g.:

a bottle of

a kilo of

a slice of

a box of

a piece of

We've got **a bottle of** water.

You need **three bottles of** water.

Can I have **a slice of** bread?

Here are **two slices of** bread.

but / however

We use *but* and *however* to contrast two things. Note the difference in punctuation.

I don't eat a lot. I still put on weight.

I don't eat a lot, **but** I still put on weight.

I don't eat a lot. **However**, I still put on weight.

Lessons 45–48

Comparatives and superlatives

1 We use a comparative to compare two people, places or things.

Karen is **older** than Mark.

After a comparative we normally use *than*.

2 We use a superlative to compare more than two people, places or things.

Salim is **the oldest** person in our class.

We must have *the* before a superlative.

This is **the** smallest restaurant.

NOT ~~This is smallest restaurant.~~

After a superlative we normally use *in*.

This is the busiest street **in** our town.

NOT ~~This is the busiest street of our town.~~

Grammar reference

Spelling

1 To make the comparative of adjectives we add *-er*. To make the superlative of adjectives we add *-est*.

young	younger	the youngest
long	longer	the longest

2 For adjectives that end in *-e*, we add *-r* or *-st*.

large	larger	the largest
nice	nicer	the nicest

3 For adjectives with a short vowel and only one consonant, we double the consonant and add *-er* or *-est*.

hot	hotter	the hottest
big	bigger	the biggest

4 For adjectives that end in *-y*, we remove the *-y* and add *-ier* or *-iest*.

busy	busier	the busiest
easy	easier	the easiest

5 For adjectives with two or more syllables (where the second syllable is not *-y*), we do not add *-er* or *-est*. We put *more* or *the most* in front of the adjective.

popular	more popular	the most popular
interesting	more interesting	the most interesting

6 Some adjectives are irregular.

good	better	the best
bad	worse	the worst
far	further	the furthest

(not) as … as

We can use *(not) as … as* to compare people, places and things.
> This café isn't **as** busy **as** that one.
> Our new neighbours aren't **as** friendly **as** our old neighbours.

too / enough

We use *too* and *enough* to say why something isn't right.
> These shoes are **too** small.
> They aren't big **enough**.
> NOT ~~They aren't enough big.~~

> This shirt is **too** short.
> It isn't long **enough**.

Lessons 49–52

Future with *will*

1 We use the future with *will* to make predictions or general statements about the future.
> In the future people **will live** on the Moon.
> We**'ll be** late for the meeting.

Positive and negative statements

I		
He		
She	'll	be late.
It	(will)	work from home.
We	won't	pay the bill.
You	(will not)	
They		

2 To make questions with *will*, we put *will* in front of the subject.

yes / no questions and short answers
Statement: We will use cash.

Question: Will we use cash?   Yes, we will.
                                  No, we won't.

wh- questions
How **will people** pay for things?
Where **will we** live?

Lessons 53–56

-ing (gerunds)

1 When we talk about an activity we normally use the *-ing* form of the verb (the gerund).
> We love **skiing**.
> NOT ~~We love ski.~~
> I've never tried **scuba-diving**.
> NOT ~~I've never tried scuba-dive.~~

2 We don't normally use an article with a gerund
> **Horse riding** is great.
> NOT ~~The horse riding is great.~~
> My favourite activity is **reading**.
> NOT ~~My favourite activity is the reading.~~

Grammar reference

First conditional

1 We use first conditionals to talk about the real or probable results of an action or event.
If you **get up** late, you**'ll miss** your bus.

2 We use the present simple in the *if* clause and the future with *will* in the main clause.
if clause   main clause
If it **rains**, we **won't go** to the beach.
NOT ~~If it will rain, we won't go to the beach.~~

3 The *if* clause can come before or after the main clause. If it comes before the main clause, we put a comma at the end of the *if* clause.
If it rains, we won't go to the beach.
We won't go to the beach if it rains.

4 *if* / *when*
We use *if* for a possible condition. We use *when* for a definite condition.
I'll phone you **if** the train is late.
I'll phone you **when** I arrive.

Time clauses

We use the first conditional form with time clauses as well as *if* clauses. Time clauses start with words such as:
before, after, when, while

We'll go swimming **before** we **have** lunch.
NOT ~~We'll go swimming before we will have lunch.~~

I'll phone him **after** the meeting **finishes**.
When the phone **rings**, I'll answer it.
They'll look after the bags **while** we **have** a meal.

Lessons 57–60

Obligation

1 We use *have to* / *has to* and *must* to show obligation.
We **have to** wait for the visitors.
Jim **has to** work on Sundays.
I **must** go to the bank.

2 *Must* and *have to* have the same basic meaning. We normally use *must* when the need comes from the speaker.
I'm hungry. I **must** have a sandwich.

We normally use *have to* when the authority comes from someone else.
I **have to** photocopy these things for the boss.

3 We use *have to* with *I*, *you*, *we*, and *they*. We use *has to* with *he*, *she*, and *it*.
I **have to** go to the meeting.
She **has to** go to the meeting, too.
Must is the same for all subjects.
I must leave.
He must leave, too.

4 The negative forms of *have to* and *must* have different meanings.
Don't / Doesn't have to means that it is not obligatory or necessary.
You **don't have to** go to work tomorrow. It's Saturday.

Mustn't means that it is not allowed.
You **mustn't** park there. It's private property.

Lessons 61–64

Subject and object questions

1 In a *wh-* question with the question words, *What* and *Who*, the question word can be the subject or the object of the verb.

2 When the question word is the object, we use the normal question structure.
What **do you do** in the house?
Who **does she meet** at lunchtime?

3 When the question word is the subject, we use a statement form of the verb.
What **wakes** you **up** in the morning?
Who **cleans** the windows?

should / shouldn't

1 We use *should / shouldn't* to give advice.
You **should** stay in bed if you're ill.
You **shouldn't** go to work.

2 *Should / Shouldn't* is a modal verb. It's the same for all subjects.
She **should** use a stepladder.
You **shouldn't** stand there.

3 *Should(n't)* is followed by an infinitive without *to*.
We **should** eat more fruit.
NOT ~~We should to eat more fruit.~~

Grammar reference

Lessons 65–68

Passives

1 These two sentences have the same meaning:
Active voice: People **take** things to the recycling centre.
Passive voice: Things **are taken** to the recycling centre.
People is the subject of the active verb.
Things is the subject of the passive verb.

2 We use the passive voice when the action is more important than who or what did it.
Things are taken to the recycling centre.

We don't know (or need to know) who takes them.

3 We make the passive voice with the verb *to be* and a past participle. With a singular subject we use *is*. With a plural subject we use *are*.
The model **is** painted.
The materials **are** recycled.

4 We can use the passive voice in any tense. To make different tenses we change the verb *to be*.
Past simple:
The model **was** painted last week.
The materials **were** recycled.

Lessons 69–72

Relative clauses

1 A relative clause gives more information about an item in a sentence.
I saw the woman.
I saw the woman **who works in the Finance Department**.

2 A relative clause starts with a relative pronoun. We use:
– *who* with people
– *which* with things and animals
– *that* with people, things, and animals.

There's the man **who** lives at number 22.
OR There's the man **that** lives at number 22.
Is this the computer **which** isn't working?
OR Is this the computer **that** isn't working?

3 A relative pronoun can be the subject or the object of a relative clause.
Is this the program? **The program** isn't working properly.

Is this the program **which** isn't working properly?

Quit the program. You're using **the program**.

Quit the program **which** you're using.

Relative pronouns are the same whether they are the subject or the object.

Lessons 73–76

Phrasal verbs

1 Some verbs in English have two parts. We call these phrasal verbs.
With some phrasal verbs the meaning is clear from the meanings of the two parts.
stand up
sit down

2 With some phrasal verbs we can't work out the meaning from the individual parts.
look after
break down

Present perfect; *for / since*

1 We use the present perfect when an activity started in the past and still continues in the present.
I**'ve worked** here for ten years. (And I still work here now.)

2 When the action finished in the past, we use the past simple.
I**'ve worked** here for ten years. (I still work here.)
Before that I **worked** in a factory for two years. (But I don't work there now.)

3 In this context we often use time expressions with *for* or *since*.

for and since	
We use *for* with a period of time	for six months for nine hours for a long time
We use *since* with a point of time.	since 1982 since February since 10 o'clock

NOTE We can't use *since* with the past simple, because it means 'from a point in the past to now'.

I've **been** here since 10.30.
NOT ~~I was here since 10.30.~~

Lessons 77–80

Adjectives with -ed or -ing

1 We use adjectives with *-ed* to describe how a person feels.

I'm **excited**. We're going on holiday tomorrow.
We were **frightened**. We watched a horror film.

2 We use adjectives with *-ing* to describe a person, place, or thing.

The holiday was **exciting**.
It was a **frightening** film.

would; second conditional

We use the conditional form *would* to talk about unlikely or unreal events.

On a perfect day **I would see** all my family.
If he had a year off, **he would write** a book.

Positive and negative statements		
I He She It We You They	'd (would) wouldn't (would not)	retire. go to work. live in the USA.

Questions

To make questions with *would*, we put *would* in front of the subject.

1 *yes/no* questions and short answers
Statement: **You would** retire.

Question: **Would you** retire? Yes, I would.
No, I wouldn't.

2 *wh-* questions
What **would you** do?
Where **would she** live?

Second conditional

1 We normally use *would* in a second conditional sentence.
Second conditionals describe unreal, unlikely, or imaginary situations.
If I **had** more time, I **would travel** round the world.

2 We use the past simple in the *if* clause and *would* in the main clause.
if clause   main clause
If I **saw** a fire, I **would phone** the fire brigade.
NOT ~~If I would see a fire, I would phone the fire brigade.~~

3 The *if* clause can come before or after the main clause. If it comes before the main clause, we put a comma at the end of the *if* clause.
If we won the lottery, we'd buy a boat.
We'd buy a boat if we won the lottery.

Audio scripts

Michael Zofia, this is my wife, Mia.
Zofia Pleased to meet you, ... sorry. What's your name again?
Mia It's Mia. M-I-A. Nice to meet you, too. Zofia.
Michael Zofia's Polish.
Mia Oh, really?
Zofia What about you, Mia? Are you Canadian, too?
Mia No, I'm not. I'm Chinese.
Zofia Oh, that's interesting.

3.1

Man OK, can I take some details then? Your first name, please?
Meryem It's Meryem. That's M-E-R-Y-E-M.
Man Uh-huh. Thank you. Now what's your surname?
Meryem It's Yilmaz.
Man How do you spell that, please?
Meryem It's Y-I-L-M-A-Z.
Man Thank you. And what's your date of birth, Ms Yilmaz?
Meryem The second of June 1980.
Man So that's oh-two, oh-six, eighty. And what's your nationality?
Meryem I'm sorry?
Man Nationality – where are you from?
Meryem Oh yes, of course. I'm from Turkey.
Man OK. Now, occupation. What do you do?
Meryem I'm a chemist.
Man I see. And are you married?
Meryem Yes, I am.
Man Have you got any children?
Meryem Yes, I have. Two – a girl and a boy.
Man Oh, how nice. Now, some contact details. What's your address, please?
Meryem It's number 55 Gleeson Road.
Man How do you spell Gleeson, please?
Meryem It's G-L-double-E-S-O-N.
Man Thank you. And is that here in London?
Meryem Yes, it is.
Man OK, and what's the postcode, please?
Meryem It's NW19 7GH.
Man Mmm-hm. And can I have a daytime telephone number, please?
Meryem Well, it's best to use my mobile number. It's oh double seven eight four, five nine three, one six two.
Man Thank you. And have you got an email address?
Meryem Yes, it's meryem.yilmaz@abc.com.
Man Thank you very much. Well I'll send you an email to confirm all these details and I'll see you soon.

8.3

1 **Woman** Hello, Abbey Dental Practice.
Caller Hello. My name's Tom Smith. I've got an appointment on the thirtieth of March at twenty past three, but I'm afraid I can't make it now.
Receptionist I see. Would you like to make a new appointment, Mr Smith?
Caller Yes, please.
Receptionist Can you come next Thursday in the afternoon?
Caller What date is that?
Receptionist It's the eighth of April.
Caller Yes, that's fine. What time?
Receptionist Well, I've got two o'clock or twenty to four.
Caller Oh, twenty to four, please.
Receptionist Fine. So your new appointment is at three forty on Thursday the eighth of April.
Caller Thank you very much. Goodbye.
Receptionist Goodbye.
2 **Receptionist** Hello, Lifestyle Therapy Centre.
Caller Hello. I've got an appointment on the twenty-seventh of January, but I'm afraid I can't make that now.
Receptionist I see. What time is your appointment?
Caller It's at ten to twelve.
Receptionist Ah, yes. Ms Clark?
Caller Yes, that's right. Could I make a new appointment, please?
Receptionist Yes, of course. Let me see. Can you come on the ninth of February in the morning?
Caller What day is that?
Receptionist It's a Monday.
Caller Yes, that's fine. What time?
Receptionist Well, I've got ten past ten or twenty-past ten.
Caller Oh, the later time, please.
Receptionist Fine. So your new appointment is at ten twenty on Monday the ninth of February.
Caller Thank you very much. Goodbye.
Receptionist Goodbye.

9.3

I get up at 7.30 and I have a shower. Then I get dressed and I make the bed. I have breakfast and I listen to the radio. Then I go to work.

I have lunch at one o'clock. After work, I sometimes go shopping or I play tennis with some friends. When I get home, I have dinner. I sometimes do some housework in the evening. I watch the news on TV and then I go to bed. I read a book for a quarter of an hour before I go to sleep.

11.1

At first life was great for me and my wife, Seema. We had two young children, and we both had good jobs. I earned a lot of money, so we had a big house.

But we weren't happy because I didn't spend much time with my family. I left home at 7.30 every morning and I didn't get home till eight o'clock in the evening. I travelled a lot in my job, too, so I was often away at weekends.

Then about five years ago, we were on holiday. It was beautiful, but I couldn't relax. I phoned my office every day. My wife wasn't happy about that.

One day we had a big argument about it, so I went for a walk on the beach. I saw a small house. There was a man in front of the house. When he saw me, he said: 'Hey! It's a beautiful day. Smile!' I stopped to talk to him.

He was a carpenter and he made furniture – beds, tables, chairs. So I said: 'Why aren't you working today?' And he said: 'Well, I made a table last week and I sold it this morning, so we've got enough money.'

That changed my life. When we got home, I left my job. We sold our big house in the suburbs and we moved to a small village in the country. I spend a lot more time with my family now. We soon knew everybody in the village, because Seema got a job as a teacher in the village school.

And me? I make furniture, but I'm not working today. I sold a table yesterday, so today I'm going fishing.

13.3

My parents were born in Chile, but I wasn't. They moved to England in the 1940s.

I was born in Liverpool in 1951. I didn't grow up in Liverpool. We moved to London when I was a baby and I grew up there.

I started school when I was five years old. I enjoyed school.

When I was sixteen I fell in love with a girl in my class. Her name was Charlotte. She was my first girlfriend and I thought she was gorgeous. I went out with her for about a year.

I left school in 1969 and I went to Birmingham University. I studied Physics there. I graduated in 1972 and I got a job with an engineering company.

My wife's name is Diana. She's Australian. I met her in Sydney. We were at a conference there.

We got married in 1980 and we had two children. Then in 1986 my company closed down and I lost my job. That was a hard time. I was thirty-five years old. I had a young family and no job.

I tried two or three other jobs, but they weren't very good. So in 2001 we moved to South Africa. We're still there now. I started my own engineering company and at the moment everything is OK.

Audio scripts

Clerk Hello. Can I help you?
Woman Yes. Could I have a ticket to Manchester, please – first class?
Clerk Are you travelling today?
Woman Yes.
Clerk Single or return?
Woman Single, please.
Clerk OK. That's fifty-two pounds, please.
Woman Thank you. What time is the next train, please?
Clerk The next train is at ten twenty-two. Change at Crewe.
Woman When is the next direct train?
Clerk It's at eleven thirty.
Woman Is that a fast train?
Clerk Yes, it is. It gets to Manchester at twelve forty-five.
Woman Oh, that's better. What platform does the eleven thirty train leave from?
Clerk Platform number six.
Woman Thank you very much.

19.1

1 **Man** ... Euston station, please.
Driver OK. The traffic's very bad this evening.
Man Yes, it is.
Driver What time's your train, then?
Man Seven forty-five.
Driver Where are you travelling to?
Man Scotland.
Driver So, is that seven forty-five the last train then?
Man Yes, it is.
Driver Right. Are you from Scotland?
Man Yes, I am.
Driver So you're going home, then.
Man Yes, I am. And my train goes in ten minutes. Are we nearly there?
Driver Yes, we are, but, like I said, the traffic's very bad. That's the station over there.
Man Oh, well, look. Can you drop me here? I can walk from here.
Driver Are you sure?
Man Yes, this is fine.
Driver OK. That's eight pounds fifty, then, please.
Man Here you are.
Driver Ten pounds. Thank you.
Man Keep the change.
Driver Thank you very much. Would you like a receipt?
Man No, thank you. I haven't got time. Goodbye.
Driver Bye.

2 **Woman** Taxi! ... The Western Hotel, please.
Driver OK. It's chilly today.
Woman Oh yes, it is, but it's a lot colder in Berlin.
Driver So, is that where you're from – Germany?
Woman Yes, it is.
Driver Are you here on holiday, then?
Woman Yes, I am. I'm spending a few days here. It's a lovely city.
Driver Yes. Are you staying at the Western Hotel?
Woman Yes, I am.
Driver Do you like it there?
Woman Yes, it's very nice, thank you.
Driver Right, well. Here we are, the Western Hotel.
Woman Thank you.
Driver That's five pounds fifty, please.
Woman Here you are.
Driver Thank you very much. Enjoy your holiday.
Woman Thank you. Goodbye.
Driver Goodbye.

3 **Man** Taxi! ... the airport, please.
Driver OK.
Here we are, the airport. Which terminal do you want?
Man Oh, I don't know. It's probably on the ticket. Just a minute. No, I can't see it.
Driver Well. Where are you flying to?
Man To Milan.
Driver Oh, well you need International Departures, then. That's Terminal 2. Terminal 1 is for domestic flights.
Man Thank you.
Driver Well, there was only one terminal till three years ago. Then they opened the new one – Terminal 2.
Man Oh, I see.
Driver So are you from Italy, then?
Man No, I'm not. I'm from Egypt. I'm going to Italy on business.
Driver Oh, right. Well, here we are - Terminal 2.
Man Thank you.
Driver That's ten pounds fifty, please.
Man Here you are. Could I have a receipt, please?
Driver Certainly. There you go.
Man Thank you. Goodbye.
Driver Goodbye. Have a nice flight.

21.3

I come out of the station and I turn right. I go under the bridge and I walk down the hill. At the bottom of the hill there's a park on the left-hand side. I usually walk through the park. In the middle of the park there's a lake. There's a bridge over the lake, but I don't usually go over the bridge. I walk round the lake. It's very nice. When I come out of the park, I turn left and I walk past the sports centre. There's a supermarket on the right hand side. Opposite the supermarket there's a small street. There's a chemist's shop on the corner of the street. My office is at the end of the street.

25.2

1 Jules and Lidia: We sailed across the Pacific Ocean from South America to Asia.
2 Pedro: I flew across Africa. I started in the Canary Islands. I flew across the Sahara Desert to Lake Victoria and I finished at the Indian Ocean.
3 Timo and Selma: We cycled across Europe from north to south. We started in the north at the Arctic Ocean and we cycled down to the Mediterranean.
4 Akane: I ran across North America. I started in New York on the Atlantic Ocean and I ran across the USA and over the Rockies to San Francisco on the Pacific.

26.2

1 **Man** Do you want to join us for drink this evening, Andy?
Andy Thanks, but I'm going to have an early night.
2 **Shana** What shall we do this evening, Omar. There's nothing on telly.
Omar Why don't we watch a DVD?
Shana Yes. OK.
3 **Man** Are you busy this evening, Rosie?
Rosie Yes, I always go to the gym on Wednesdays.
4 **Martina** Bye. And don't be late this evening, Bruno.
Bruno Why not?
Martina Don't you remember? The meal with Audrey and James.
5 **Bradley** Can I use the computer this evening? I want to send some emails.
Woman Sure, Bradley.
6 **Roy** What shall we do this evening, Emma?
Emma Let's play tennis.
Roy Oh yes. Great idea.

Audio scripts

27.1

Presenter With me this morning are Rachel Morgan from Wales and Stefan Popko from Poland. In October they're going to take part in the Global Challenge race. So Rachel, what is this race?

Rachel We're going to sail round the world in a yacht.

Presenter When people normally sail round the world, they go from west to east.

Rachel Yes. That's because the wind goes from west to east. We're going to sail east to west against the wind.

Presenter So Stefan, where are you going to go?

Stefan We're going to sail down the Atlantic Ocean to Argentina. Then round the bottom of South America and across the Pacific Ocean to New Zealand. From there we're going to sail across the Indian Ocean to South Africa and then home.

Presenter Phew, and how long is that going to take?

Stefan We're going to travel over fifty-six thousand kilometres. That's going to take about a hundred and fifty days.

Presenter And how many people are going to be in the race?

Rachel There are going to be twelve yachts with eighteen people on each yacht. They're going to be from all over the world.

Presenter And how big are the yachts?

Stefan They're about twenty-two metres long, so with eighteen people it's going to be very tight. We can only take one kilo of luggage each.

Presenter One kilo? So the question is … Why are you going to do it?

Stefan Because we want to.

29.2

1 **Woman** Hi, Imran. How's your new boss?
Imran Oh, she's OK.
Woman What does she look like?
Imran Well, she's quite slim. She isn't very tall.
Woman How old is she?
Imran I don't know – She's middle-aged.
Woman What's her hair like?
Imran Er, she's got medium-length hair.
Woman Straight?
Imran Oh, er, no. She's got wavy hair and it's very dark. She's quite pretty, actually.

2 The police are looking for a man in connection with the robbery. They describe the suspect as quite young, medium height and a bit overweight. He's got very curly, fair hair and blue eyes. He's also got a small moustache. Anyone who sees the man should phone the police on …

32.2

1 **B** Excuse me.
A Yes. Can I help you?
B Yes. How much are these sports bags, please?
A The small ones are thirty-two euros and the large ones are fifty euros.
B Can I have a look at one of the small ones, please?
A Certainly. Here you are. We have them in black or green.
B It's very nice, but it's a bit small.
A Would you like to see one of the large ones?
B Yes, please.
A Here you are.
B Thank you. Yes. I think I prefer the large one. I'll take it.
A Black or green?
B Oh, the green one, please. How much is it again?
A Fifty euros. Anything else?
B No, thank you.
A That's fifty euros, then, please.

2 **A** Can I help you?
B Yes. You've got some earrings in the window. Can I have a look at them, please?
A Can you show me? These ones?
B Yes, and the ones next to them. Yes, those ones.
A OK. Here you are.
B How much are they, please?
A The gold ones are a hundred and fifteen euros and the silver ones are seventy-two euros.
B I like the gold ones, but I think I prefer the silver ones.
A Yes, they're very nice.
B Yes, … but no. I'll take these ones, please.
A The gold ones?
B Yes.
A Anything else?
B No, thank you.
A That's a hundred and fifteen euros, then, please.

33.2

1 **A** What kind of programmes do you normally watch, Bob?
B Well, I don't watch TV a lot, but I always watch the news and the weather forecast. I like documentaries, too, you know like *Our World* and things like that.
A Do you watch any reality TV shows, like *The House*?
B No, I don't like them. What about you? Do you watch a lot of TV, Anna?
A Yes, I suppose, I do. I watch a lot of game shows. My favourite is *Lucky Chance*.
B Do you like soap operas?
A Yes. I always watch *Beacon Street*.
B Do you watch any sports programmes?
A No, I don't like sport.

2 **A** What sort of things do you watch on TV, Julie?
B I watch a lot of sitcoms, mostly American ones like *Jack and Jennie*. I love that. I like hospital dramas, too. *Emergency* is my favourite hospital drama.
A Do you watch the news?
B No, I never watch the news or documentaries or things like that. My parents always watch them, but I've got my own TV, so it's not a problem. What things do you usually watch on TV, Ivor?
A I usually watch films. I like chat shows, too – like *The Ronnie Melbourne Show*.
B Do you watch any soaps or sitcoms?
A No, I don't.

35.1

This is the news with Martin West. The headlines:

The heads of government of the EU countries have arrived in Budapest for their latest meeting.

Thieves have stolen gold and a large number of diamonds from a bank in Paris.

A tropical storm has hit the coast of South America. Strong winds have destroyed several villages. More than a hundred people have lost their lives.

Two people have died in a fire at a factory in Glasgow.

And some news has just come in. There has been a serious accident on the M5 motorway. A small plane has crashed into a bridge. The police have closed the motorway in both directions between junctions 5 and 7. We have no more information at the moment.

The game show *The Box* has won the Independent award for the best radio programme of the year.

Alan Jones, star of the TV sitcom *The Avenue* has married the programme's writer, Rajni Sekar.

That's all the news for now. More on that accident on the M5 and all the other stories in our next bulletin at nine o'clock. And now the weather forecast … .

Audio scripts

1 **A** What's the matter?
 B I've got a headache.
 A Oh, dear. Here, I've got some painkillers.
 B Thanks.
2 **A** What's wrong?
 B I've hurt my wrist. It's swollen.
 A Oh, yes, it is. Put some ice on it.
 B Yes, that's good idea. Thanks.
3 **A** What's wrong?
 B My arm itches.
 A Oh, yes. You've got a rash on it. Here. I've got some cream for it.
 B Oh, thanks.
4 **A** What's the matter?
 B My nose is bleeding.
 A Oh, yes. Here, I've got some tissues.
 B Thank you.
5 **A** What's the matter?
 B I've cut my hand.
 A Oh, dear. Here, I've got some plasters.
 B Thank you.
6 **A** What's wrong?
 B I've burnt my finger.
 A Oh, dear. Here, put it under the cold water.
 B OK. Thanks.

38.3

1 **A** What have you done to your elbow, Kathy?
 B I've sprained it.
 A How did you do that?
 B I fell downstairs.
 A Really? When did it happen?
 B On Thursday.
2 **A** Hi, John. What have you done to your leg?
 B I've cut my knee.
 A How did you do that?
 B I dropped a knife on it in the kitchen. I was wearing shorts.
 A Oh, dear. When did it happen?
 B Yesterday morning.
3 **A** What have you done to your arm?
 B I've bruised my elbow.
 A How did you do that?
 B I hit it against the car door.
 A Ooh, that sounds bad. When did it happen?
 B Two days ago.

40.2

1 **Doctor** Good morning. Now what seems to be the problem?
 Patient My ear hurts.
 Doctor I see. Which ear is it?
 Patient My left ear.
 Doctor When did it start?
 Patient Oh, about two days ago now. Yes, it started on Monday morning.
 Doctor Well, can I just have a look at it? Hmm, yes, it's a bit red in there. I think you've got an infection.
 Patient Oh, I see.
 Doctor Take this medicine – one capsule four times a day.
 Patient OK.
 Doctor If it isn't any better by Friday, come back and see me.
 Patient Yes, OK. Thank you. Goodbye.
 Doctor Goodbye.
2 **Doctor** Good morning. Now what can I do for you?
 Patient I've hurt my elbow.
 Doctor Your right elbow?
 Patient Yes.
 Doctor I see. Can I just have a look at it? Hmm, yes it's swollen. How did you hurt it?
 Patient I banged it on a desk at work yesterday.
 Doctor I see. Well, I think you've just bruised it, but we'd better get an X-ray. Take this letter to the hospital.
 Patient OK.
 Doctor In the meantime, put some ice on your elbow and take some painkillers.
 Patient Yes, OK. Thank you. Goodbye.
 Doctor Goodbye.

41.3

A Are you ready to order?
B Yes. Can I have the grilled salmon, please?
A What kind of potatoes would you like – baked, boiled, or chips?
B Oh, boiled, please.
A And what would you like with that?
B Oh, can I have roasted vegetables, please?
A OK so that's grilled salmon with boiled potatoes and roasted vegetables.
B Thank you.

47.1

1 Peter: I usually go to the local shops in the town centre. It's friendlier and more personal. Last year I went to the supermarket for some wine, but the assistants didn't know anything except the price. Now I always go to a small wine shop in the town centre. It isn't as cheap as the supermarket, but the man there knows a lot about wine.
2 Susan: When I was a child there were a lot of local shops. There was a baker's, a butcher's, and a greengrocer's. But then they built a big supermarket near the town. Now all the small shops have gone. Well, you can understand it. They weren't as convenient as the supermarket. So we have to go to the supermarket now – at least the parking is easier there.
3 Anjit: I always shop at the supermarket because it's more convenient. The shops in the town are only open from nine to five thirty and I'm at work then. They're closed on Sundays, too. The supermarket's open longer hours and every day. And you can buy everything at one shop.
4 Birgit: I go to the local shops and the market because I think the food is fresher. If I go to the supermarket, the tomatoes are from South Africa and the lettuce is from India. Why do we bring food from the other side of the world when you can get it from a local farm?
5 Troy: I usually shop on the Internet because I can shop twenty-four seven. I order food and things on the Internet and the supermarket delivers everything to my house. It's the easiest way to shop and it's cheaper, too.

Audio scripts

1 **Customer** Excuse me. Have you got these shoes in a size five, please?
Assistant Just a minute. ... Yes, here you are.
Customer Thanks. I'll just try them on.
Assistant How are they?
Customer They're too loose. Have you got them in a smaller size?
Assistant Just a minute. No. I'm sorry. That's the smallest size.
Customer Oh, OK. Thanks anyway.
2 **Customer** Excuse me. Can I try this jumper on, please?
Assistant Yes. The changing rooms are over there.
Customer Thank you.
Voice *Later*
Assistant How is it?
Customer It isn't big enough. It's too tight on the chest. Have you got it in a larger size?
Assistant What size is that?
Customer Small.
Assistant Do you want to try a medium?
Customer Yes, please.
Assistant OK. Just a minute. Yes. Here you are.
Voice *Later*
Assistant Is that big enough?
Customer Yes. This is more comfortable, thanks. I'll take it.
Assistant Anything else?
Customer No, thanks.
Assistant OK. Well, if you'd just like to come to the till ...
3 **Customer** Excuse me. How much are these jeans, please?
Assistant They're sixty-two pounds.
Customer Can I try them on, please?
Assistant Sure. The changing rooms are over there.
Customer Thank you.
Voice *Later*
Assistant How are they?
Customer They're too short. Have you got them with a longer leg?
Assistant Just a minute. Yes. Here you are. Try these.
Customer Thanks.
Voice *Later*
Assistant Do they fit better?
Customer Yes. These are long enough, thanks. I'll take them.
Assistant Anything else?
Customer No, thanks.
Assistant That's sixty-two pounds then, please.

1 **A** That's nineteen pounds twenty, please.
B Oh, dear. I haven't got enough money. I've only got seventeen pounds.
2 **A** That's sixteen pounds and nine pence, please.
B Here you are.
A I'm sorry we don't take credit cards.
B Oh.
3 **A** We need to get a ticket at the machine.
B Yes, have you got any coins? I haven't.
A No, I haven't either. I've only got notes.
4 **A** This is nice.
B Yes, it is, but I can't buy it. I haven't had my salary this month yet.
5 **A** Oh, erm ...
B What's the matter?
A I can't remember my PIN. Is it six eight ... no six nine ... ?
6 **A** Thank you. That's two pounds change.
B Excuse me. I gave you a twenty-pound note. You've only given me change for ten pounds.
A Oh? Oh, yes, you're right. Sorry about that. Here you are.
7 **A** Dad, can I borrow some money?
B No, I lent you some money last week, and you haven't given it back.
A But I've spent it.
8 **A** What's this? I paid this bill last week.
B Well, they've sent your cheque back. You didn't sign it.

1 Hello, Kay. Your visitors phoned. Their plane was late, so they won't arrive before three o'clock. OK? Bye.
2 Good morning, Kay. This is Farida in Mexico. I've got the photographs. I'll email them to you today. Bye for now.
3 Hello, darling. I'm sorry, but I won't have time to book the theatre tickets. Can you do it? Thanks. Bye. Oh, I left the money for the cleaner in the kitchen.
4 Hi, Kay. This is John Morgan. I'm still in Paris, so I'm afraid I'll miss the meeting this afternoon. See you.
5 Hello, dear. It's your mother. I want to talk to you about your father's birthday. I'll phone you later. Bye. She isn't there. It's one of those answer phone things, you know.
6 Hello. This is the computer engineer. I'm sorry, but I won't have time to fix your computer today, so I'll fix it tomorrow morning. Bye.
7 Hey, Mum. I'm going to a party tonight, so I won't need a meal. Oh, and I've borrowed some money. It was in the kitchen. Hope that's OK.
8 Hello, Mrs Winter. It's Margaret, the cleaner. I can't find my money, and I won't be here next week. I'll be on holiday. So I really ...

Beth What do you like doing in your free time, Arnold?
Arnold I like water-skiing.
Beth Really?
Arnold Yes, and I like sailing, too.
Beth Do you like canoeing?
Arnold It's OK. I don't mind it.
Beth Have you tried scuba-diving?
Arnold No, I haven't. I like being on the water, but I don't like being under it.
Beth Oh, I see. What do you do when you aren't on the water?
Arnold Not a lot. I like relaxing in the garden, listening to music. You know – doing nothing really.
Beth Do you like doing DIY?
Arnold No, I don't. I'm not very good at it. Anyway, what about you? What do you like doing?
Beth Well, I like swimming.
Arnold Oh right. So have you tried scuba-diving, then?
Beth No, I haven't, but I'd like to. It looks great. So what else? Urm ... I like playing tennis.
Arnold Uh-huh. Are you any good?
Beth Yes, not bad. But I'm not really into exercise. I don't like going to the gym or jogging.
Arnold Oh, I see.
Beth I don't mind doing yoga, but I suppose most of all I like going out with friends. You know, going to restaurants, shopping, things like that.
Arnold Oh, right, so what's your favourite restaurant?

119

Audio scripts

1 **Receptionist** Good morning, the Angel Hotel. You're speaking to Vicky. How may I help?

Caller Hello. I'd like to book a room, please.

Receptionist Certainly sir. When for?

Caller For the twenty-fifth of April, please for two nights.

Receptionist Two nights. And is it just one room?

Caller Yes, it is.

Receptionist Just one moment, sir. Yes, that's OK. How many guests is it for?

Caller Just myself.

Receptionist And would you like a single, a double, or a twin room, sir?

Caller A single, please. And I'd like a non-smoking room, if you have one, please.

Receptionist Yes, we do. So that's a single room – non-smoking – for two nights from the twenty-fifth of April.

Caller Yes, that's it.

Receptionist That will be sixty pounds per night.

Caller Does that include breakfast?

Receptionist No, I'm afraid it doesn't. That's for the room only, sir.

Caller OK.

Receptionist What name is it, please?

Caller It's Carlos Gonzalez.

Receptionist Is that G O N Z A L E Z?

Caller Yes.

Receptionist Thank you, and do you have a credit card to confirm the booking?

Caller Yes. It's …

2 **Receptionist** Hotel Jumbo. Buon giorno.

Caller Oh, hello. I'd like to make a reservation, please.

Receptionist Certainly, madam. When for?

Caller For the sixth of November, please.

Receptionist How many nights?

Caller Just one night, please.

Receptionist One moment, please. And how many guests?

Caller Two – myself and a friend.

Receptionist And would you like a double or a twin room?

Caller A twin room, please.

Receptionist Yes, that's fine. We have a twin room for the sixth of November.

Caller We'd like a room with a balcony, if you have one, please.

Receptionist Erm. Yes, we do. So that's a twin room with a balcony for the sixth of November – just one night.

Caller Yes, that's right.

Receptionist That will be one hundred euros per night – bed and breakfast.

Caller Thank you.

Receptionist What name is it, please?

Caller It's Carol Mills. That's M I double L S.

Receptionist Thank you, and can I take a credit card number to confirm the booking?

Caller Yes, of course. It's …

Sayeed Hello Josh.

Josh Hi, Sayeed. How are you?

Sayeed Fine, thanks. How was your day today?

Josh It was OK.

Sayeed What did you do?

Josh Well, when I got to work I made a few phone calls and I sent some emails. I had a break at about eleven and then I went to a meeting.

Sayeed Uh-huh.

Josh After lunch I made a couple of appointments for next week. Then I did some filing and I went on the Internet. So a normal day really. What about you, Sayeed? How was your day?

Sayeed Oh, I worked at the weekend, so I had a day off today.

Josh Lucky you. So what did you do, then?

1 I live in a small town near Venice and I work in the city centre. I travel into the city by train. I live near the station so I don't have to drive. I take the train to the central station in Venice, and from the station I get the Vaporetto or waterbus to St Mark's Square. The journey takes about an hour and a half from my home to my office. It's OK, but in the summer the waterbus is very crowded with tourists.

2 I live in the suburbs of Kuala Lumpur in Malaysia. Every morning I have to travel into the city centre where I work. A few years ago the journey took over two hours because the traffic was very bad. But now we have a monorail metro. It's very fast and comfortable and I can read the newspaper or a book. Unfortunately, I don't live near the metro station, so I have to get a bus to the station. The journey only takes about an hour and a quarter now, so I don't have to get up very early.

3 I live and work in New York – in Manhattan – and I usually cycle to work. It's fast and it's good exercise, too. The journey takes about half an hour. I wear shorts or sweatpants and a sweatshirt and I have to take my clothes in a bag. Then I have a shower when I get to work. Problems? I can't cycle in winter, so I have to take the subway then, but that takes about forty-five minutes. Car drivers are the biggest problem. They open doors in front of you and things like that. So you have to be very careful.

1 **Assistant** Hello. Can I help you?

Customer Yes, I bought this jumper at the weekend, but it's got a hole in it.

Assistant Oh, yes. I'm sorry about that. Would you like to exchange it?

Customer Yes, please.

Assistant Just a moment. … . Here you are. This one's OK.

Assistant Thank you.

2 **Assistant** Hello. Can I help you?

Customer Yes, I bought this kettle two days ago, but there's something wrong with it.

Assistant I see. What's the problem?

Customer It's leaking.

Assistant Oh? I'm sorry about that. Would you like to exchange it?

Customer No, thank you. Can I have a refund, please?

Assistant Yes, of course. Have you got the receipt?

Customer Yes. Here you are.

Assistant Thank you.

3 **Assistant** Hello. Can I help you?

Customer Yes, I bought this clock radio on Monday, but it's damaged. Look.

Assistant Oh, yes. I'm sorry about that. Would you like to exchange it?

Customer Yes, please.

Assistant Just a moment. … I'm sorry that was the last one. We should have some more next week.

Customer Oh, well can I have a refund then, please?

Assistant OK. Have you got the receipt?

Customer Yes. Here you are.

Assistant Thank you.

4 **Assistant** Hello. Can I help you?

Customer Yes, I bought this CD yesterday, but it's scratched.

Assistant I see. Would you like to exchange it?

Customer Yes, please.

Assistant Have you got the receipt?

Customer Yes. Here you are.

Assistant Just a moment, then, please … . Here you are. This one should be OK.

Customer Thank you.

65.3

Reporter I'm at the recycling centre, and I'm talking to Arthur Collins. What materials can people recycle here?

Arthur We recycle a lot of materials – glass, paper, plastic, metal. We collect wood, too, and cardboard.

Reporter I see. What things do most people bring to the recycling centre?

Arthur Most people recycle newspapers and magazines, glass bottles – and plastic bottles, too.

Reporter I can see some metal cans over there.

Arthur Yes, people bring cans – and cardboard boxes, too.

Reporter Are those things easy to recycle?

Arthur Yes, they are. The biggest problem is with things like televisions and computers, because they're made of a lot of different materials – plastic, glass, rubber, metal. Some of the metals are very expensive, like silver and gold.

Reporter I see. So what do you ...

66.2

The model in this picture was built one sixth of normal size. I can't show you the model, because it was destroyed for a TV programme. It was made from wood and paper. The buildings and streets were built first. Then the small things were added. Children's toys were used for things like bicycles and plants. Shop signs were painted by hand. These small things are very important. When the model was seen on TV, people thought it was real. The street was used in a history programme. It was shown on TV last year.

67.1

1 I'm from Thailand. My favourite festival is Loy Krathong. It's celebrated at the end of the rainy season. It's to say thank you for the water. Small boats are made from banana leaves. A candle, flowers, and coins are put in the boat. In the evening, people take their boats to the nearest river, canal, or lake. The candles are lit and the boats are pushed out onto the water. It looks really beautiful. We believe that our bad luck is taken away by the boats, so we feel happy.

2 The Day of the Dead is one of the biggest festivals in Mexico. It's celebrated on the second of November every year. It's when dead friends and relatives are remembered. Big models of skeletons are made from paper, wood, and cardboard. These skeletons are carried through the streets. Small skeletons are eaten, too – but these are made from sugar and bread. They're sold in shops and markets. In their houses, people have flowers, candles, food, and photographs of their dead friends and relatives. We remember the good times with them.

3 My favourite festival here in Russia is Maslenitsa. It's celebrated at the end of winter. Winters are very long and cold in Russia, so we're all happy when it finishes. For the festival a model of a woman is made from straw. It's dressed in women's clothes. This is Lady Maslenitsa. There are lots of parties and people visit their relatives. And – this is the best part for the children – they eat lots of pancakes. They're delicious. At the end of the week, Lady Maslenitsa is burnt and we say goodbye to winter.

69.3

A Right, what's open on your desktop at the moment?
B It's a file.
A Well, save that.
B OK. I've saved it.
A What program are you using?
B Word.
A OK. Quit that.
B Right. I've done that.
A Good. Now can you see the icon for your email?
B Yes, I can.
A Fine. Click on it.
B OK. I've done that.
A Is your email window open now?
B Yes. It's the inbox.
A All right. Now scroll down to the email with the attachment and click on it.
B OK. The email is open now.
A Right. Now go to the menu bar and click on Edit. You should see the menu ...
B Well, I've done all that.
A Good. Now click OK and restart your computer. It should be fine.

72.2

1 **Katrin** John. I need something for my hairdryer. What do you call the thing that you put in the wall?
John A plug.
Katrin A plug?
John Yes. Do you want a plug for your hairdryer?
Katrin No, it's got a plug, but it isn't the plug that you use here in England.
John Oh, I see. You need an adaptor.
Katrin An adaptor. Yes. Have you got an adaptor for this plug?
John No. I'm sorry. But why don't you use Sally's hairdryer and we can get an adaptor tomorrow.
Katrin Oh, OK.

2 **Katrin** This is a photo of my brother.
Sally What does your brother do?
Katrin Oh ... what do you call someone who builds things?
Sally Do you mean someone who builds houses? A builder?
Katrin No. He builds offices, bridges, and things like that.
Sally Oh, he's a civil engineer.
Katrin Sorry?
Sally A civil engineer. It's two words: Civil. That's C-I-V-I-L, and then the next word – engineer.
Katrin Oh, right, a civil engineer.

3 **Katrin** What do you call the part where you type on a computer?
John The keyboard. The things that you press are the 'keys', so the whole thing is a keyboard.
Katrin How do you spell that?
John K-E-Y-B-O-A-R-D.
Katrin Keyboard. OK.

73.3

1 A Hello, Mike.
B Oh, hi, Mary. Come in. Please sit down.
2 A Why are you putting on your jacket?
B I'm going out.
3 A Is that your neighbours' dog?
B Yes, I always look after it when they go away.
4 A Have you switched off your mobile?
B I'm looking for it now. I can't find it.
5 A Can you stand up, please? I can't find my keys.
B Just a minute. I'll switch on the light. There they are.

74.2

1 A How long have you worked here?
B I've been here for nearly three years.
2 A How long have you been a policeman?
B I've been in the police since 2003.
3 A How long were you and Jim married?
B Only three years.
4 A Have we lived in France for three years or four years?
B We've been here for three years.
5 A Did you work at the bank for a long time?
B I worked there for eight years.

Audio scripts

Paul Helen, it's good to see you.
Helen Yes, and you, Paul. How are you?
Paul Great, thanks. And you?
Helen Fine. Are you married?
Paul Yes, I've been married for nine years and we've got three children.
Helen Oh, lovely. What do you do? Didn't you get a job at a bank after university?
Paul Yes, I'm still there, but I'm a manager now.
Helen Where do you live?
Paul In Manchester. We've been there for three years. We've got a nice house in the suburbs and Georgina – that's my wife – teaches at a local school. What about you?
Helen Oh, well, when I left university, I got a job with an insurance company, but I didn't like it, so I was only there for six months.
Paul What did you do?
Helen I travelled to Australia, south-east Asia, and Canada.
Paul Great! What did you do there?
Helen I worked on farms, in hotels, in shops – and I met my husband! His name was Troy and he played the trumpet in a band.
Paul Wow. Cool.
Helen Yes, I was a singer with the band for a couple of years. It was fun but then I wanted to do the normal thing – get a real job, buy a house, have children. But Troy didn't.
Paul So, what happened?
Helen We got divorced and I came back to England. I've been back for four years now. I work for a computer company.
Paul In London?
Helen Yes. I share a flat with a friend there.
Paul I always wanted to travel and play the guitar in a band.
Helen Yes, but you've got a good job, a nice house, a family. You've got all the things that I've always wanted.
Paul But you've done all the things that I wanted to do. That's life, eh?

1 **A** I've got an interview tomorrow.
  B Are you worried?
  A Yes, I am.
2 **A** Oh, no!
  B What's the matter?
  A I'm annoyed. My laptop isn't working.
3 **A** *Yawn!*
  B Are you tired?
  A Yes, I am.
  B Have you had a busy day?
  A No, I was at a party last night.
4 **A** I'm going to get a pizza. I'm hungry. I didn't have any lunch.
5 **A** There's nothing on TV. I'm really bored.
6 **A** Our son has won a school prize.
  B That's great. I bet you feel proud.
  A Yes, I do.
7 **B** Hi, Mark. How are you?
  A I'm fine. I had a day off today. I feel really relaxed.
8 **A** Just a minute. When's the meeting – this week or next? ... I'm confused!

Sarah It's true, Ryan. Russell didn't know anything about Anna and Starlight Properties.
Ryan Anna and what? I'm talking about the car. He didn't put any petrol in it.
Cindy Yes, the car just stopped in the middle of the road. It was very embarrassing.
Ryan And when we finally got to the solicitor's, they were closed. You stupid boy!
Peter Closed? So you didn't sign the contract?
Cindy No, we didn't.
Jordan You haven't sold the café?
Ryan No, we haven't. And it's all Russell's fault.
Lucy Oh, that's great! It's wonderful news!
Cindy Wonderful? What are you talking about, Lucy?
Peter Sit down. We'll tell you all about it.

Voice Later ...
Jordan So, that's it.
Ryan That's amazing. Thank you very much. You've saved The Coffee Shop.
Sarah Well Russell helped, too. You didn't get to the solicitor's because he didn't put any petrol in the car.
Cindy Oh, yes. You clever boy, Russell. Well done.
Russell Thanks, Mum.
Ryan Oh, I don't believe it!

Irregular verbs

Verb	Past simple	Past participle
be	was / were	been
beat	beat	beaten
become	became	become
begin	began	begun
bet	bet	bet
bite	bit	bitten
blow	blew	blown
break	broke	broken
bring	brought	brought
build	built	built
burn	burnt / burned	burnt / burned
buy	bought	bought
can	could / was able to	been able to
catch	caught	caught
choose	chose	chosen
come	came	come
cost	cost	cost
cut	cut	cut
dig	dug	dug
do	did	done
draw	drew	drawn
drink	drank	drunk
drive	drove	driven
eat	ate	eaten
fall	fell	fallen
feel	felt	felt
fight	fought	fought
find	found	found
fly	flew	flown
forget	forgot	forgotten
get	got	got
give	gave	given
go	went	been/gone
grow	grew	grown
have	had	had
hear	heard	heard
hide	hid	hidden
hit	hit	hit
hold	held	held
hurt	hurt	hurt
keep	kept	kept
know	knew	known
lead /liːd/	led	led
learn	learnt / learned	learnt / learned
leave	left	left

Verb	Past simple	Past participle
let	let	let
lose	lost	lost
make	made	made
mean	meant	meant
meet	met	met
pay	paid	paid
put	put	put
quit	quit	quit
read /riːd/	read /red/	read /red/
ride	rode	ridden
ring	rang	rung
run	ran	run
say	said	said
see	saw	seen
sell	sold	sold
send	sent	sent
set	set	set
shake	shook	shaken
show	showed	shown
shrink	shrank	shrunk
shut	shut	shut
sing	sang	sung
sit	sat	sat
sleep	slept	slept
smell	smelt / smelled	smelt / smelled
speak	spoke	spoken
spell	spelt / spelled	spelt / spelled
spend	spent	spent
stand	stood	stood
steal	stole	stolen
stick	stuck	stuck
sweep	swept	swept
swim	swam	swum
swing	swung	swung
take	took	taken
teach	taught	taught
tell	told	told
think	thought	thought
throw	threw	thrown
understand	understood	understood
wake	woke	woken
wear	wore	worn
win	won	won
write	wrote	written

Pronunciation chart

iː /siː/ see	**ɪ** /sɪt/ sit	**ʊ** /pʊt/ put	**uː** /tuː/ too
e /bed/ bed	**ə** /əbaʊt/ about	**ɜː** /tɜːn/ turn	**ɔː** /sɔː/ saw
æ /kæt/ cat	**ʌ** /ʌp/ up	**ɑː** /fɑːðə/ father	**ɒ** /hɒt/ hot

ɪə /nɪə/ near	**eɪ** /deɪ/ day	⟋⟍→
ʊə /pjʊə/ pure	**ɔɪ** /bɔɪ/ boy	**əʊ** /gəʊ/ go
eə /ðeə/ there	**aɪ** /maɪ/ my	**aʊ** /haʊ/ how

p /pen/ pen	**b** /bæd/ bad	**t** /tiː/ tea	**d** /dɔː/ door	**tʃ** /tʃeə/ chair	**dʒ** /dʒæm/ jam	**k** /kæn/ can	**g** /get/ get
f /faɪv/ five	**v** /væn/ van	**θ** /θɪn/ thin	**ð** /ðə/ the	**s** /sɪt/ sit	**z** /zuː/ zoo	**ʃ** /ʃuː/ shoe	**ʒ** /juːʒəli/ usually
m /mæn/ man	**n** /nɒt/ not	**ŋ** /sɪŋ/ sing	**h** /hæt/ hat	**l** /leg/ leg	**r** /red/ red	**w** /wet/ wet	**j** /jes/ yes

OXFORD
UNIVERSITY PRESS

Great Clarendon Street, Oxford OX2 6DP

Oxford University Press is a department of the University of Oxford.
It furthers the University's objective of excellence in research, scholarship,
and education by publishing worldwide in

Oxford New York

Auckland Cape Town Dar es Salaam Hong Kong Karachi
Kuala Lumpur Madrid Melbourne Mexico City Nairobi
New Delhi Shanghai Taipei Toronto

With offices in

Argentina Austria Brazil Chile Czech Republic France Greece
Guatemala Hungary Italy Japan Poland Portugal Singapore
South Korea Switzerland Thailand Turkey Ukraine Vietnam

OXFORD and OXFORD ENGLISH are registered trade marks of
Oxford University Press in the UK and in certain other countries

ISBN: 978 0 19 430727 7

Printed in China

ACKNOWLEDGEMENTS

*The author would like to thank all the people at Oxford University Press who have
contributed their knowledge, skills, and ideas to producing this book.*

*The author would like to dedicate this book to his sister, Shiela, and his brothers,
Colin and Pat.*

Commissioned photography by: Gareth Boden: pp1, 14, 42, 75

Illustrations by: Stuart Briers: p 71, Stefan Chabluk: p 69, Cyrus Deboo: pp 5, 9,
21, 24, 29, 32 (objects), 37 (objects), 39, 49, 57 (office activities), 73, 87; Mark
Duffin: pp 25, 26, 58, 97, Paul Fisher Johnson: p 23, Tony Hall: pp 5 (cartoons),
13, 30, 31, 37, 65, 77, Sarah Kelly: pp 4, 8, 32, 41, 56, 64, 72, 80, 93; Chris
Pavely: pp 11, 16, 22, 48, 57, 61, 62, 85, 89, Roger Penwill: p 46, 78, 91, Klaus
Trommer/Storyboards.nl: pp 4, 6, 10, 12, 18, 20, 26, 28, 34, 36, 38, 44, 50, 52,
58, 60, 68, 70, 74, 76, 81

Story page illustrations by: Klaus Trommer/Storyboards.nl

*We would like to thank the following for permission to reproduce the following
photographs:* Advertising Archive p 33 (TV Advert), AKG Images p 33
(Lucasfilm/20th Century Fox/ALB/Star Wars, Alamy pp 1 (Stephen Oliver/
girl with long hair), 45 (David R. Frazier Photolibrary/Music shop/Sports
shop, Andrew Fox/Flower shop, Stephen Roberts/Hardware shop), 47 (Jon
Arnold Images/High Street), 53 (Brandon Cole Marine Photography/scuba
diving, Vic Pigula/canoeing. Ianni Dimitrov/sunbathing, Chris Howes/
Wild Places Photography/DIY, David R. Frazier Photolibrary/painting, Art
Kowalsky/sightseeing), 54 (Photo Japan/cherry blossom, Stock Connection
Distribution/man, Art Kowalsky/ beach), 65 (Frank Chmura/paper), Allstar
pp 33 (Warner Brothers/Friends, 20th Century Fox/The Simpsons cartoon),
Art Directors and Trip pp 1 (man in white shirt), Catherine Blackie p 45
(travel Agent) Bosch p 61 (washing machine, dishwasher, microwave, kettle,
toaster, vacuum cleaner), BBC Documentary 'Hiroshima' © The Model Unit
p 66 BBC Photograph Library pp 33 (News, weather, Police, hospital, chat
show, game show), Bubbles p 63 (man changing nappy), Nicky Clarke p 61
(hairdryer), Corbis Images pp 3 (Kevin Dodge/woman on phone), 15 (Ray as
young man) 27 (Malcolm Hanes/yacht), 35(Matthias Kulka/diamonds, Chuck
Savage/man with prize), 45 (Richard Klune/butcher, Birgid Allig/Greengrocer,
John Dakers/Jewellery shop), 47 (Gideon Mendel/supermarket), 51 (Dave
Amit/floods), 55 (Paul Barton/yoga, Amos Nachoum/scuba diving), 59
(Viviane Moos/kuala Lumpur), 63 (H. Schmid/washing machine), 65 (Patrik
Engquist/Etsa/wood, Serge Kozak/zefa/plastic, cotton, 67 Danny Lehman/The
Day of the Dead Festival), 99 (bonfire), Daikin p 61 (air conditioner), De
Longhi p 61 (desk fan), DK Images pp 59 (bicycle), 65 (silver, glass, rubber
tyre, belt), Fremantle Media Stills p 33 (Neighbours), Gamma pp 45 (Neema
Frederic/Furniture shop), Getty Images pp1 (Kaz Chiba/man with necklace,
Nobuko Shiga/Acollection/man in tie, Siri Stafford/woman in orange, 7
(David A Land/man with red hair, AFP/ oil rig), 19 (Yellow Dog Productions),
27 (Scott Barbour/Brighton Rally), 35 (Robert Sullivan/hurricane damage), 51
(Daniel Berehulak/Virgin Galactic), 53 (Andy Whale/water-skiing, Antonio
Mo/friends), 54 (Andreas Kindler/ girl), 55 (Southern Stock/yacht), 65 (Jake
Wyman/metal, Gianni Cigolini/gold, DK Images/cardboard/leather bag,
Keren Su/wool, Derek P Redfearn/slipper), 79 (Car Culture/ sports car),
95 (David Hume Kennerly/market), 101 (Catherine Ledner/man tousled
hair, LWA/woman black hair, Gregory COstanzo/woman red hair, Jacobs
Stock Photography/man white shirt, Sally and Richard Greenhill pp 27
(marathon), Eye Ubiquitious p 45 (Chemist), Kent News & Pictures p 33
(reality TV show), Kobal Collection pp 15 (Universal/boy at piano, Nobo
Heating p 61 (heater), Oxford University Press pp 3 (Punchstock/man on
computer), 43 (Punchstock), 45 (Punchstock/baker), 47 (Punchstock/market),
53 (Punchstock/relaxing/girl on computer) 67 (Punchstock/Loy Krathong
festival) 71 (Getty Images), 83 (Digital Vision), Philips p 61 (radio clock,
DVD player, razor, light bulb), Photofusion pp 1 (David Mondford/Olga), 53
(Stuart Saunders/gym), PA Photos pp 27 (John Stillwell/boat race), 45 (George
Widman/department store), 51 (Pat Roque/masks), 53 (Horst Ossinger/
clubbing), 55 (Leslie Mazoch/AP/salsa), 67 (Mikhail Metzel/ Maslenitsa
Festival), 79 (SportsChrome/sky diving), Pulse Photo Library p 40 (Julian
Claxton/Chemist) Reuters p 51 (Jacky Naegelen/soldiers), Rex Features pp
15 (Ray Charles in red shirt), 17, 33 (football, polar bears), 45 (Newsagent,
Estate Agent, Hairdressers, Stationers), 47 (Shopping on Internet), 51 (tiny
computer), 53 (mountaineering, sailing, ducks), 59 (vaporetta), Science Photo
Library p 40 (CC Studio/doctor)

The photographs on page 66 are from the BBC Documentary 'Hiroshima' ©
The Model Unit

Thanks to Executive Producer Matthew Barrett for permission for their use.